MARINE
DIESEL ENGINES

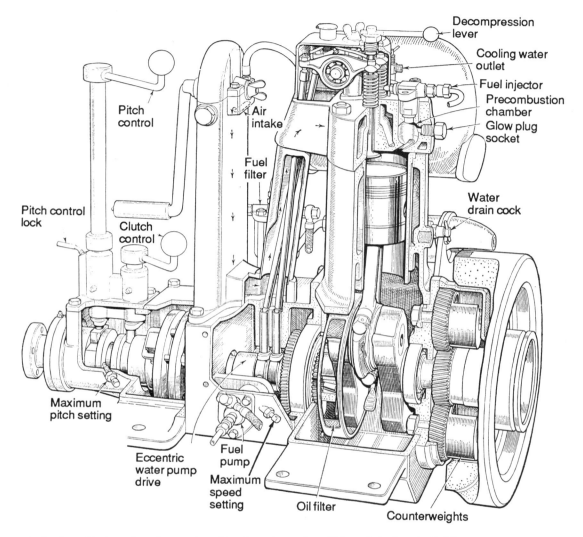

Decompression lever

Cooling water outlet

Fuel injector

Precombustion chamber

Glow plug socket

Pitch control

Air intake

Fuel filter

Pitch control lock

Clutch control

Water drain cock

Maximum pitch setting

Eccentric water pump drive

Fuel pump

Maximum speed setting

Oil filter

Counterweights

A single cylinder, 4-cycle marine diesel engine of traditional design (a Sabb type G, 10 h.p., courtesy of Sabb Motor A.S.). This illustration shows clearly the principal components to be found in any diesel engine.

MARINE DIESEL ENGINES

Maintenance, Troubleshooting, and Repair

Nigel Calder

International Marine Publishing Company
Camden, Maine

Published by International Marine Publishing Co., a division of Highmark Publishing, Ltd., 21 Elm Street, Camden, Maine 04843.

Typeset by Typeworks, Belfast, Maine.
Printed and bound by Rand McNally, Taunton, Massachusetts.

10 9 8 7 6 5 4 3 2

Library of Congress Number 87–2918
ISBN Number 0-87742-237-0

To Terrie,
who never minds getting grease under her fingernails

Contents

Preface

This book provides the basic information necessary to select, install, maintain, and carry out repairs on a marine diesel engine. It is neither a simple how-to book nor a technical manual on the thermodynamics of internal-combustion engines. Rather, it falls somewhere between the two.

This reflects my own experience as a self-taught mechanic with some 20 years' experience on a variety of engines, from 10 to 2,000 h.p. With specific enough instructions it is perfectly possible to dismantle an engine and put it back together again without having any understanding of how it works. Troubleshooting that engine without a basic grasp of its operating principles, however, is not possible.

In order to grasp these operating principles, just a little of the most basic theory behind internal-combustion engines—more than found in many how-to books—is all you really need to know. It is also possible to be a whiz at theory and a useless mechanic. You'll find not a single intimidating mathematical formula in this book. What I have tried to do is present the general theory underlying diesel engine operation, but only what is necessary to provide a good understanding of the practical side of diesel engine maintenance. My objective is to help turn out competent amateur mechanics, not automotive engineers.

This particular blend of theory and practical mechanics represents a mix that·has worked well for me over the years. Although my approach may help the boat owner see trouble coming and nip it in the bud before his engine breaks down, it may leave some readers hungry for more theory. To them, I'll suggest the library; it contains numerous books that deal in great depth with all aspects of thermodynamics.

Although this book has been written with engines from 10 to 100 h.p. in mind, the principles are virtually the same as those associated with engines of hundreds or even thousands of horsepower. The information in this book applies to just about all diesels.

Sources of data and drawings are indicated throughout the book, but I would, nevertheless, like to thank all those who have helped me, in particular, Paul Landry and Bill Osterholt for their many suggestions, and the companies that provided drawings and other help. They are: Borg Warner Automotive, Caterpillar Tractor Co., the AC Spark Plug Division of General Motors, ITT/Jabsco, Lucas CAV Ltd., Perkins Engines Ltd., Pleasurecraft Marine Engine Co., Sabb Motor A.S., Garrett Automotive Products Co., Volvo Penta, Holset Engineering Co. Ltd., and United Technologies Diesel Systems.

I extend my thanks to Dodd, Mead and Company for permission to use the material from Francis S. Kinney's *Skene's Elements of Yacht Design,* and to Reston Publishing Company for information contained in Robert N. Brady's *Diesel Fuel Systems.*

Dennis Caprio, my editor, has made a mass of detailed suggestions that have improved this book greatly. Jonathan Eaton at International Marine has always been helpful and encouraging. Any errors remaining are solely mine.

Nigel Calder
Ponchatoula, Louisiana
June 1986

Introduction

For very good reasons the diesel engine is now the overwhelming choice for sailboat auxiliaries, and it is becoming more popular in sportfishing boats. Diesels have an unrivaled record of reliability in the marine environment; they have better fuel economy than gasoline engines; they are more efficient at light and full loads; they emit fewer harmful exhaust pollutants; they last longer; and they are inherently safer because diesel fuel is far less volatile than gasoline.

Despite its increasing popularity, the diesel engine is still something of a mystery, propagated in large part by the differences that distinguish it from the gasoline engine. The first objective of this book, then, is to explain how a diesel engine works, to define new terms, and remove the veil of mystery.

If the owner of a diesel engine has a thorough understanding of how it works, then he will fully grasp the necessity for certain crucial aspects of routine maintenance and the expensive consequences of habitual neglect. Properly maintained, most diesel engines will run for years without trouble, which leads to my second objective—to drive home the key areas of routine maintenance.

If and when problems arise, they normally fall into one or two easily identified categories, and your knowledge of how the engine works will be the key to troubleshooting the problem. My third objective is to outline troubleshooting techniques that promote a logical, clearheaded approach to solving the problem.

The fourth section of the book goes through various maintenance, overhaul, and repair procedures that can reasonably be undertaken by an amateur mechanic, and one or two that should not really be attempted but which might become necessary in a dire emergency. Major mechanical breakdowns and overhauls are not included. This kind of work can only be carried out by a trained mechanic.

The book is rounded out with a consideration of correct engine installation procedures and some criteria to assist in the selection of a new engine for any given boat. Much of the last section may throw some light on problems with an engine already installed.

There is no reason for a boat owner not to have a long and troublefree relationship with a diesel engine. He only needs to pay attention to routine maintenance, have the knowledge to spot early warning signs of impending trouble, and have the ability to correct small problems before they become large ones.

MARINE
DIESEL ENGINES

Chapter One

Principles of Operation

To understand the operation of a diesel engine, you must know a little bit about heat, pressure, and the behaviour of gases in a sealed chamber.

Heat

All solids, liquids, and gases (all "bodies") contain heat to a greater or lesser extent. Theory states that to remove all heat from a body it would have to be cooled to minus 460°F, a temperature known as *absolute zero*. This is a purely theoretical calculation that has never been achieved in practice. The higher the temperature above −460°F, the more heat a body contains. This quantity of heat can be measured. The unit of measurement is not degrees Fahrenheit or Celsius (centigrade), but something called British thermal units (Btus).

One Btu is defined as the quantity of heat required to raise the temperature of one pound of water one degree Fahrenheit. Therefore, adding 20 Btus to one pound of water will raise the temperature from 140°F to 160°F. The removal of 20 Btus will cool it back down to 140°F.

The Btu is used to measure *quantities* of heat; the thermometer measures the *intensity* of the heat of a body, what we perceive as feeling cold or hot, but the temperature of a body tells us very little about how much heat it contains. A one-ton block of iron at 90°F will feel the same as a 10-pound block at the same temperature, but the one-ton block will contain 200 times more Btus of heat energy than the 10-pound block.

Pressure

Pressure is commonly measured in pounds per square inch absolute (psia) and pounds per square inch gauge (psig). Any measurement in pounds per square inch gauge (psig) is 14.7 pounds lower than the same measurement in pounds per square inch absolute (psia). In other words, psig = psia − 14.7. From where do we get 14.7?

Atmospheric pressure. The earth is surrounded by an envelope of gases (air, the atmosphere). Although we have no sensation of weight, these gases do in fact have weight. Imagine a pile of 10 books, one atop the other. The top two or three might only weigh a pound or so, but farther down the stack the cumulative weight of books is a great deal more.

It is just the same with the atmosphere. The outer layers bordering on space weigh almost nothing and exert very little downward pressure. At sea level, however, the accumulated mass of the atmosphere exerts a pressure of 14.7 pounds per square inch on the surface of the earth. This pressure decreases by approximately 0.5 psi with every 1,000 feet of altitude.

1

Gauge and absolute pressure. Because we are born and raised in this atmosphere, it becomes the norm for us, and we have no sensation of the pressure it exerts—we are adjusted to an ambient pressure of 14.7 psi. It therefore makes sense to calibrate pressure gauges to zero at atmospheric pressure, and then they will register any deviation from the ambient pressure. This is what is meant by pressure per square inch *gauge* (psig, commonly abbreviated to psi). On the other hand, a gauge which is calibrated to measure the real, or actual, pressure will have to register 14.7 psi at atmospheric pressure. This is what is meant by pressure per square inch *absolute* (psia).

Vacuum. Let us imagine taking our two gauges into space. As we rise higher into the Earth's atmosphere, the pressure steadily decreases. When we finally enter deep space, the gauge calibrated in pounds per square inch absolute will read zero—a perfect vacuum. What about the other gauge? It has been calibrated to read zero when the pressure is actually 14.7 psi. Now, as we reach true zero, this gauge will have to read minus 14.7 psi, but in practice another scale is used to indicate readings below atmospheric pressure. This is inches of mercury (abbreviated to Hg). A perfect vacuum (−14.7 psi) is equivalent to −29.2 inches of mercury, and this is what the gauge will read in deep space. In other words, 30 inches Hg is roughly equivalent to 15 psi. Therefore a pressure one pound below atmospheric pressure will show −2 inches Hg; 5 pounds below atmospheric pressure, −10 inches Hg; and so on.

Pressure measurements in engine work are made almost exclusively in pounds per square inch gauge, or psi. Because parts of an engine commonly fall below atmospheric pressure (e.g., the engine air-inlet manifold on many engines), it is sometimes necessary to deal with partial vacuums. Generally speaking the only time that absolute pressure is introduced is when considering the effects of high altitude on engine performance.

Gases

If a gas is put in a sealed cylinder and then the volume of the cylinder is reduced (e.g.,

by forcing a piston up one end) two things happen: the pressure increases, and the temperature rises. The rise in temperature is not due to the addition of heat; it results from the concentration of the heat already in the gas into a smaller space. In other words, after compression the gas contains the same amount of heat (Btus) as before compression, but these Btus have been squeezed into a smaller space, creating a rise in temperature *(sensible heat)*. A somewhat loose analogy could be drawn from putting a heater in a large room and a similar heater in a small room. The small room will become hotter even though the two heaters put out the same number of Btus, because this heat is concentrated into a smaller space.

The relationship between rising pressure and temperature when a gas is compressed is a direct one. A given rise in pressure will create a given rise in temperature. The corollary also holds true: if a gas is heated in a sealed chamber, its pressure rises with its temperature. When an unconfined gas is heated it expands, but when expansion is prevented, the pressure rises.

These relationships between pressure and temperature also hold in reverse. If the pressure of a gas is reduced, its temperature will fall in direct proportion, and if its temperature is reduced, its pressure will drop in direct proportion.

The diesel engine

All engines, gasoline or diesel, consist of one or more cylinders closed off at the top with a cylinder head. Beneath the cylinder is a *crankshaft*, so called because of its offset pin and cheeks that make up the crank. A *connecting rod* ties the crankshaft to a piston that moves up and down in the cylinder. The connecting rod has a bearing at each end, and these allow it to rotate around a pin in the piston *(piston pin* or *wrist pin)* and the crank. As the piston moves up and down, the crankshaft turns (see Figure 1-3).

Most engines contain the following basic components: inlet and exhaust valves at the top of the cylinder to allow gases in and out at specific times; levers known as *rockers* to

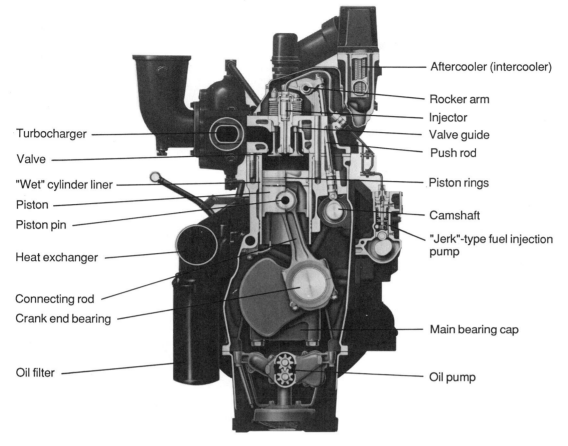

Aftercooler (intercooler)
Rocker arm
Injector
Valve guide
Push rod
Turbocharger
Valve
"Wet" cylinder liner
Piston rings
Piston
Piston pin
Camshaft
"Jerk"-type fuel injection pump
Heat exchanger
Connecting rod
Crank end bearing
Main bearing cap
Oil filter
Oil pump

Figure 1-1. *Cutaway view of a modern turbocharged diesel engine—the Caterpillar 3406B in-line 6. (Courtesy Caterpillar Tractor Co.)*

open the valves; *push rods* to push up one end of the rockers; springs located under the end of each rocker opposite the push rod to close the valves; and a shaft with elliptical protrusions on it called *cams*. As this camshaft rotates, the high point of the cam moves the push rod up, which pushes on the rocker and opens the valve. When the camshaft rotates to the low point of the cam, the valve spring pushes up on its end of the rocker, closing the valve and forcing the push rod down. The camshaft is driven by the crankshaft so that the opening and closing of the valves can be precisely coordinated, or timed, with the movement of the piston in the cylinder (see Figure 1-4).

In some engines, the camshaft is located within the cylinder head atop the valves and rockers. The cams act directly on the rockers, and the engines have no push rods. These engines are known as overhead camshaft types.

In order to ensure that the piston makes a gastight seal against the side of its cylinder, it is given a number of spring-tensioned rings that push out against the cylinder wall. These are *piston rings*. The cylinder itself is either a machined bore in a cast-iron block or a sleeve, or liner, pushed into the block. Water contained in a space called the water jacket circulates around the sleeve to keep it cool. In diesel engines, two types of sleeve are used: a wet liner, which is in direct contact with the cooling water and merely engages the block at its top and bottom where it is sealed off; and a dry liner, which is in contact with the block at all points (see Figure 1-5).

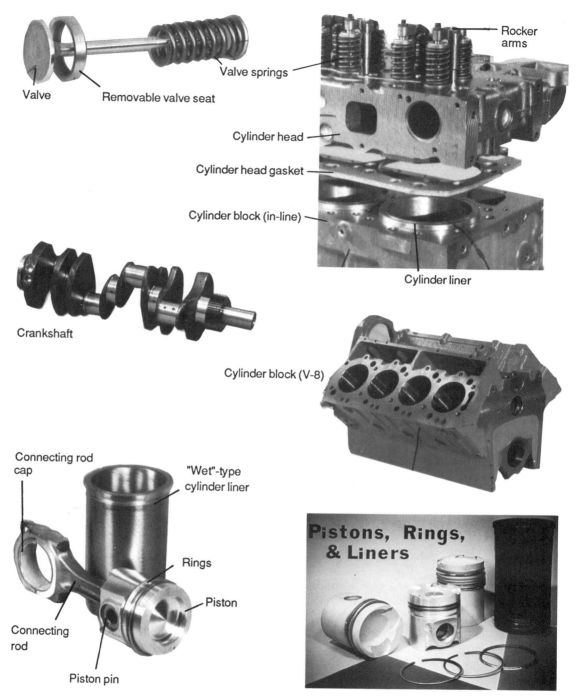

Valve

Valve springs

Removable valve seat

Rocker arms

Cylinder head

Cylinder head gasket

Cylinder block (in-line)

Cylinder liner

Crankshaft

Cylinder block (V-8)

Connecting rod cap

"Wet"-type cylinder liner

Rings

Piston

Connecting rod

Piston pin

Pistons, Rings, & Liners

Figure 1-2. *Engine parts. (Courtesy Caterpillar Tractor Co.)*

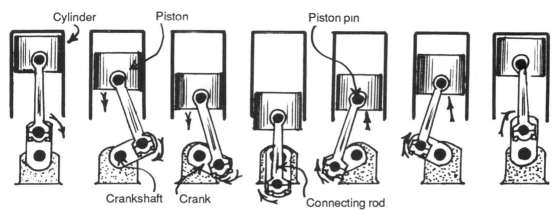

Figure 1-3. *Converting reciprocal motion to rotary motion.*

And last, in a gasoline engine a spark plug is located in the top of the cylinder; in a diesel engine its place is taken by a *fuel injector.*

Diesel engines are either 4-cycle or 2-cycle. The differences will become clear in a moment. Let us first look at a 4-cycle engine.

4-cycle diesel

1. Starting with the piston at the top of its cylinder, the inlet valve opens. The crankshaft turns, pulling the piston down the cylinder, which creates a partial vacuum. This causes air to be sucked into the cylinder (see Figure 1-6).

2. When the piston reaches the bottom of the cylinder, the inlet valve closes, which traps the air that has been drawn into the cylinder. This completes the first, inlet, stroke of the four cycles. (A stroke is the movement of the piston from the top to the bottom of its cylinder, or vice versa.)

3. The piston is now pushed back up its cylinder by the crankshaft, compressing the trapped air. As pressure rises, so too does the temperature. With the piston back at the top of its cylinder, pressure in a diesel engine's combustion chamber is raised to 500 psi or more, and this in turn raises the temperature of the compressed air in the cylinder to 850 to 1,200 °F. This completes the second, compression, stroke of the four cycles.

4. Diesel fuel is sprayed into the cylinder through the injector. The intense heat of the compressed air in the cylinder causes the fuel to catch fire. No ignition system is required, which is one of the principal differences from a gasoline engine. The burning fuel increases the temperature in the cylinder, which raises the pressure of the gases even higher, generally by around 250 psi.

5. The increased pressure pushes the piston back down the cylinder. For the first time the piston is pushing the crankshaft and

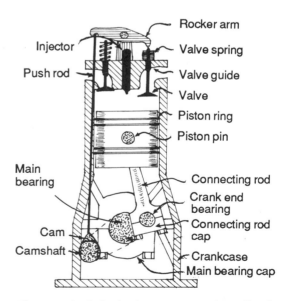

Figure 1-4. *Principal components in a diesel engine.*

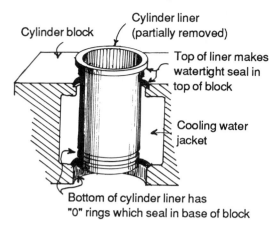

Figure 1-5. *A "wet" cylinder liner.*

not the other way around. This is the third, power, stroke of the 4-cycle engine. As the piston moves down the cylinder, it rapidly increases the volume of the cylinder, causing the pressure to fall, which causes the temperature to decrease.

6. When the piston reaches the bottom of the cylinder, the exhaust valve opens, and as the piston comes back up the cylinder (pushed by the crankshaft once again), it forces all of the burned gases out the exhaust. This is the fourth, exhaust, stroke.

7. When the piston reaches the top of the cylinder once again, the exhaust valve closes, the inlet valve opens, and we are back at the beginning of the four cycles.

2-cycle diesel

A 2-cycle engine operates in basically the same fashion, but the processes are condensed into two strokes of the piston, once up and once down the cylinder, instead of four. Here's how it works.

1. Begin with the power stroke. The piston is at the top of its cylinder, which is full of hot compressed air. The fuel is injected, and ignites. The rising temperature and pressure drive the piston back down the cylinder (see Figure 1-7).

2. As the piston moves down, pressure and temperature fall in the cylinder. When the piston nears the bottom of its stroke, the exhaust valves open. (Two-cycle engines generally have two exhaust valves per cylinder,

for reasons which will be explained later.) Most of the exhaust gases rush out of the cylinder.

3. Just after the exhaust valves open, and as the piston continues to move down (still on its first stroke), it uncovers a series of holes, or ports, in the wall of the cylinder. The exhaust valves are still open. Fresh air under pressure is blown in through these ports, driving the last of the exhaust gases out of the exhaust valves and filling the cylinder with clean air.

4. The piston has now reached the bottom of the cylinder and is on its way back up. As it moves, it blocks off the inlet ports, and at about the same time the exhaust valves close, trapping the new charge of fresh air in the cylinder. Compression begins.

5. The piston is driven to the top of the cylinder by the crankshaft, compressing the air, the diesel fuel is injected, and the cycle starts over. The piston has traveled once down the cylinder and once up.

A diesel engine produces power only when it is burning fuel. It is possible both to calculate the heat content in Btus of the fuel burned and to figure the Btu equivalent of the horsepower produced (1 h.p. = 2,544 Btus). In a perfect engine all the heat from the burning fuel would be converted into useful energy; as the piston descended on the power stroke, the pressure and temperature in the cylinder would decrease to exactly the same values that existed at the beginning of the cycle.

In practice, considerable heat and pressure remain at the end of the power stroke, and must be removed to enable a fresh charge of air to be drawn in and to prevent the build-up of dangerously high temperatures that would damage the engine. The net result is that the average diesel engine converts into usable energy just 30 to 40% of the heat generated. The rest is dissipated as cooling water, 25%–30%; exhaust gases, 25%–30%; and internal friction, radiation from the engine block, and related losses, 10%. As bad as this sounds, it is still considerably more efficient than a gasoline engine.

CYCLE 1

CYCLE 2

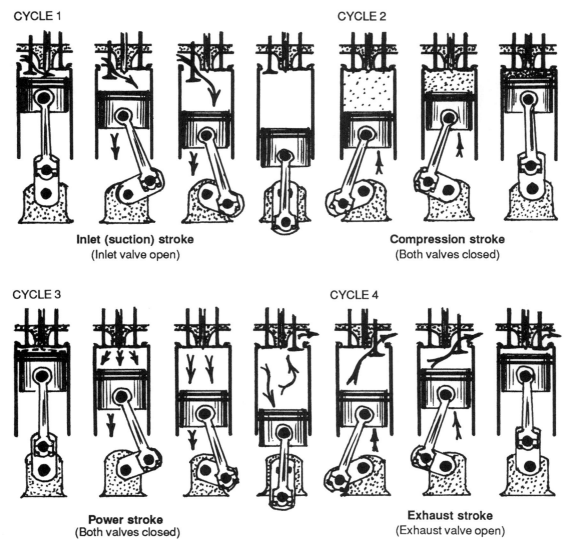

Inlet (suction) stroke
(Inlet valve open)

Compression stroke
(Both valves closed)

CYCLE 3

CYCLE 4

Power stroke
(Both valves closed)

Exhaust stroke
(Exhaust valve open)

Figure 1-6. *Operation of a 4-cycle engine.*

As previously mentioned, the diesel engine has no ignition system. The injected fuel is ignited by the temperature rise associated with compressing air to a high pressure. The ignition point of diesel fuel is about 750 °F, but in practice, most diesel engines compress the air until a temperature of about 1,000 °F is achieved.

Compression ratio is the term used to describe the degree to which the air charge is compressed in the cylinder. Specifically, it indicates the volume of the cylinder when the piston is at the bottom of its stroke relative to the volume of the cylinder when the piston is at the top of its stroke. For example, a compression ratio of 16 to 1 (generally written as 16:1) tells us that when the piston is at the bottom of its stroke the cylinder has a volume 16 times greater than when the piston is at the top of its stroke—the inlet air is being compressed to one-sixteenth its original volume.

The minimum practical compression ratio to raise the inlet air temperature sufficiently for combustion is around 14:1 (see Figure 1-9), and most modern small diesel

CYCLE 1

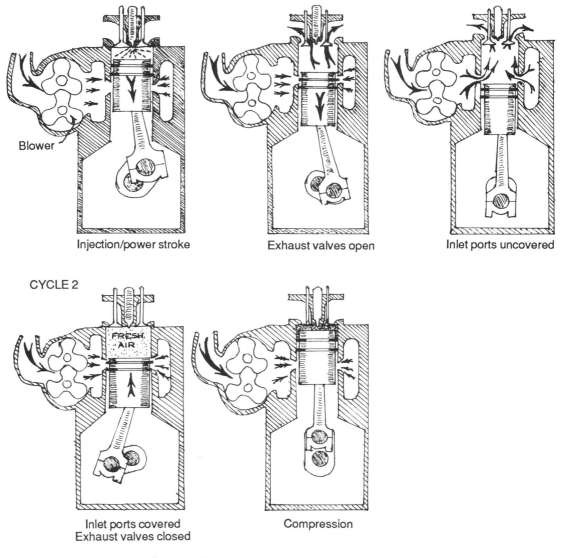

Figure 1-7. *Operation of a 2-cycle engine.*

engines of the kind under discussion here have compression ratios of 17:1 to 23:1. This is in sharp contrast to gasoline engines, which generally have compression ratios of around 7:1 to 9:1, resulting in compression pressures of 80 to 130 psi.

It is this difference in compression ratios that principally accounts for the increased efficiency of a diesel engine over a gasoline engine, for it means that the gases of com-

bustion have a greater degree of expansion on the power stroke. The more gases expand, the more they cool, which is to say that a diesel engine converts a greater proportion of the heat of combustion into useful work than does a gasoline engine—a diesel engine is more "thermally efficient."

The *rate* that thermal efficiency increases as compression ratios are increased, however, slows down. At some point, the prob-

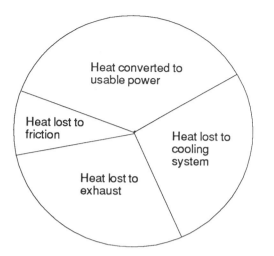

Figure 1-8. *Heat utilization of a diesel engine.*

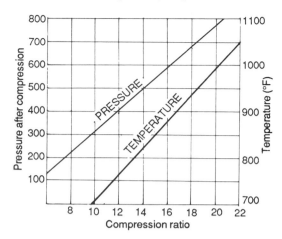

Figure 1-9. *Approximate temperatures and pressures at different compression ratios.*

lems created by the extra stresses outweigh the benefits of additional thermal efficiency, and this probably occurs close to a compression ratio of 20:1.

Why not increase the compression ratio, and therefore the thermal efficiency, of gasoline engines? The answer is that on a gasoline engine the fuel charge is drawn in through the carburetor with the air, and is compressed with it. A higher compression ratio would cause ignition to occur before the piston reached the top of its stroke, rapidly destroying the engine. Compression ratios must be kept low enough to prevent the temperature from reaching the ignition point. Then, at the appropriate moment, a spark ignites the air/fuel mixture—which is why gasoline engines have an ignition system.

You may think that fuel injection on gasoline engines could be made to serve the same function as fuel injection on diesel engines, allowing much higher compression ratios to be used and therefore considerably improving the efficiency of the engine. Gasoline, however, is far more volatile than

diesel fuel, and if injected into the super-pressurized and heated air found in a high compression engine would explode forcefully enough to damage the engine. Although it is hard to visualize in an engine turning over at 3,000 revolutions per minute (r.p.m.) with a combustion period for each power stroke of less than 0.01 second, the injected diesel fuel is burning at a controlled rate rather than exploding, which substantially reduces the shock loads on the engine. (If the fuel does indeed fail to burn at the correct rate, problems result, as we shall see later.)

The high compression ratios of a diesel engine subject all the many components to loads that are greater than those in a gasoline engine. As a result, diesel engines have to be far more solidly constructed, which accounts for the increased weight and cost of most diesel engines over gasoline engines of the same power output. In recent years, however, tremendous advances in metallurgy and engine design have enabled drastic weight reductions to be achieved on many diesels, considerably narrowing this power-to-weight gap.

Chapter Two

The Air Supply

Air is composed of about 23% oxygen by weight (21% by volume). The rest is nitrogen and other gases. The idea of air having weight is sometimes a little hard to grasp, but if you refer back to the definitions of absolute and gauge pressure in Chapter 1 you will recall that at sea level the atmosphere exerts a pressure of 14.7 psi on the earth's surface. This pressure is created by the accumulated weight of the air surrounding the earth. At sea level, and at 60°F, one cubic foot of air weighs approximately 0.076 lb. When the temperature rises, air expands, and the weight of a cubic foot of air decreases. This is of some significance for the operation of diesel engines.

Oxygen is the only component of air that is active in the combustion process of an engine—the burning of diesel fuel is actually a chemical reaction between the oxygen in the air and hydrogen and carbon in the fuel. The hydrogen combines with oxygen to form water; the carbon combines with oxygen to form carbon dioxide and, on occasion, carbon monoxide. These chemical reactions release a considerable amount of light and heat.

Although diesel fuels vary somewhat in their composition, in general about 3.36 lbs. of oxygen are required to completely burn 1 lb. of diesel fuel. Given that air is only 23% oxygen by weight, this means that approximately

$$3.36/23 \times 100 = 14.5 \text{ lbs.}$$

of air is needed to burn a single pound of fuel. If, at the atmospheric pressure of 14.7 psi and at 60°F, a cubic foot of air weighs 0.076 lb., our 14.5 lbs. of air translates into

$$14.5/0.076 = 190 \text{ cubic feet of air.}$$

If diesel fuel weighs about 7.5 lbs. per U.S. gallon, we need

$$190 \times 7.5 = 1,425 \text{ cubic feet}$$

of air to burn that one gallon. At higher temperatures, higher altitudes, or both, air is less dense and even larger volumes are needed to burn a gallon of diesel.

You won't have to remember any of these figures—the purpose in setting them down is to impress upon you *the huge quantities of fresh air required for the effective operation of a diesel engine.*

The weight of air that can be drawn into a diesel engine more or less determines its power output. Broadly speaking, more air pulled in equals more fuel burned and more heat generated, which results in more power from the engine. Engineers must do everything possible to avoid restricting the flow of air to the engine. Large air filters are generally fitted to increase the surface area through which the air is drawn; air inlet pipes and manifolds are designed with as few bends as possible; and on 4-cycle engines the inlet valves are made as large as can be accommodated in the cylinder head, while on 2-cycle engines the inlet ports are given a substantial area. The unavoidable inefficiencies created by the remaining friction in the air intake system are known as *pumping losses*. (Pumping losses include frictional losses in the exhaust system—more on this later.)

The effectiveness with which an engine draws in air is measured by a concept called *volumetric efficiency*. From the bottom of its stroke to the top, a piston occupies, or displaces, a certain volume. This is known as its *swept volume*. If an engine were to draw in enough air on the inlet stroke to completely fill this swept volume at atmospheric pressure, it would have a volumetric efficiency of 100%. Volumetric efficiency, then, is the proportion of the volume of air drawn in by the piston relative to its swept volume at atmospheric pressure.

On a standard 4-cycle engine, the downward movement of the piston on the inlet cycle reduces the pressure in the cylinder and pulls air into the cylinder. Strictly speaking, reduced pressure in the cylinder causes the higher atmospheric pressure on the outside to *push* air into the engine, but it is easier to visualize it as the piston sucking in air. Owing to friction in the air filter, inlet passages, and valves, the air pressure in the cylinder is a little below atmospheric pressure during the inlet stroke. As the air rushes into the cylinder, however, it gains a momentum of its own, and as a result of this momentum when the piston reaches the bottom of its stroke and starts to move back up on the compression stroke, air continues to enter the cylinder. To take advantage of this momentum, inlet valves are set to close a short time after the piston has started its compression stroke. The same valves are also set to open a short time before the piston has reached the top of its stroke on the exhaust cycle. This ensures that the valves are wide open by the time the piston begins its inlet stroke, which enables it to start drawing in air immediately. These measures allow most diesel engine manufac-

turers to achieve a volumetric efficiency of around 80% to 90% (see Figure 2-1).

The kind of engine that we have been considering draws in air by the action of the piston and is known as *naturally aspirated*. By taking a naturally aspirated engine and forcing more air into it, a great deal more fuel can be burned and a great deal more power generated without any increase in the engine size. This is the principle of *supercharging* and *turbocharging*.

When an engine is supercharged, a fan or blower, mechanically driven by the engine, forces air into the air inlet (see Figure 2-2). By raising the pressure of the fresh air entering the engine, a volumetric efficiency of more than 100% can be achieved—the pressure of fresh air in the cylinder at the end of the inlet stroke is increased to more than atmospheric pressure. This additional air in the cylinder means that more fuel can be in-

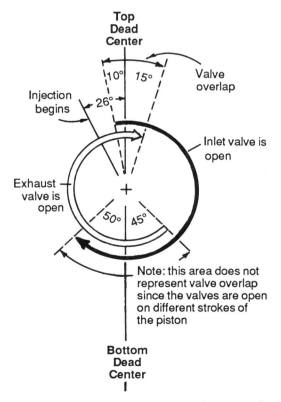

Figure 2-1. *Typical timing circle for a 4-cycle engine.*

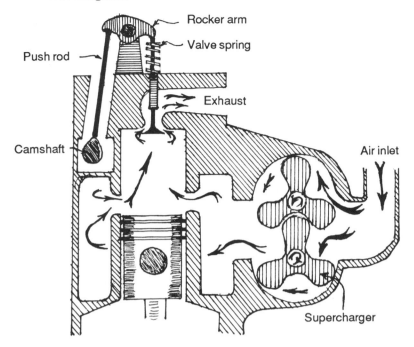

Figure 2-2. *A typical supercharger.*

jected and burned, and the engine will develop more power.

Supercharging is not employed on any small 4-cycle engines, but it is widely used on 2-cycle engines. If you refer back to the description of a 2-cycle engine in Chapter 1, you will see that when the piston is at the bottom of its stroke and the inlet ports and exhaust valves are open, pressurizing the inlet air forces all the exhaust gases out the exhaust valves. In 2-cycle engines the concept of volumetric efficiency goes under the name *scavenging efficiency.* If the fresh air drives out all the exhaust gases and completely refills the cylinder, the engine has 100% scavenging efficiency.

Turbocharging is similar to supercharging, except that the inlet air blower is driven by the engine's exhaust gases. This is accomplished by installing a fan, or *turbine*, in the exhaust passage. As the exhaust gases blow out of the engine, they spin this turbine, which is connected by a shaft to a second one installed in the air-inlet passage. This second turbine blows fresh air into the engine (see Figure 2-3). The great thing about a turbo-

charger is that if the load on an engine increases, more fuel is injected to generate more power, and this leads to more exhaust gases to spin the turbines faster and cause more air to be forced into the air inlet. The turbocharger forces up the power of the engine just when it is needed most. Turbocharging is becoming increasingly common.

Turbocharging has drawbacks, of course. The increase in exhaust back pressure caused by the turbocharger interferes with the removal of the exhaust gases from the engine, which adds to pumping losses. There is a very definite limit to the loads that a turbocharger can place on an engine without its becoming counterproductive.

Raising the pressure of the inlet air also raises its temperature by as much as 150°F, which reduces its density and lessens the weight of extra air being driven into the cylinder. For this reason many turbocharged engines have a water-cooled air inlet manifold between the turbocharger and the inlet valves. This cools off the turbocharged air by up to 90°F, which increases the density (weight) of the air entering the cylinder. This

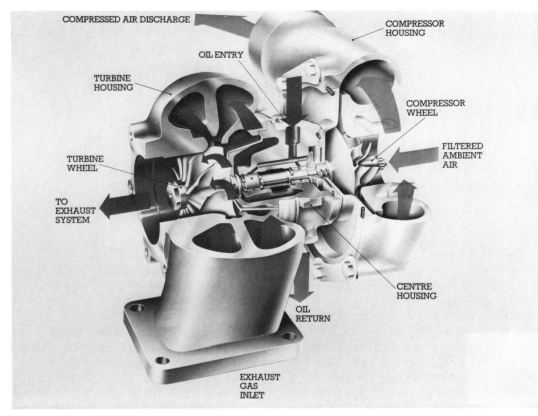

COMPRESSED AIR DISCHARGE

COMPRESSOR HOUSING

OIL ENTRY

TURBINE HOUSING

COMPRESSOR WHEEL

TURBINE WHEEL

FILTERED AMBIENT AIR

TO EXHAUST SYSTEM

CENTRE HOUSING

OIL RETURN

EXHAUST GAS INLET

Figure 2-3. *Cutaway view of a turbocharger. (Courtesy Garrett Automotive Products Co.)*

is known as *intercooling* or *aftercooling*. On some turbocharged engines the intercooler is part of the engine's cooling circuit, in which case the water passing through it is already warm. On other engines a separate water supply is provided in order to cool the turbocharged air by the maximum possible amount. This produces the maximum possible power from a given engine size.

Turbochargers add considerable complexity and expense to an engine, especially if an intercooler is also fitted, as is more and more the trend today. The additional power generated accelerates engine wear; the costs of servicing tend to be higher. On the other hand, a turbocharged engine develops up to 50% more power than a naturally aspirated engine of the same size. Even after allowing for the additional weight of the turbocharger and associated equipment, this represents a substantial increase in the power-to-weight ratio, something of concern to most boat owners.

Chapter Three

Combustion

When diesel fuel is injected into a cylinder containing high-pressure superheated air, it does not explode—it burns. This is one of its advantages over gasoline. The relatively slow burning of diesel fuel produces a more even rise in cylinder temperature and pressure than does gasoline, exerting a more gradual force on the piston over the whole length of its power stroke. As a result, diesel engines have far more constant torque (the turning force exerted by the crankshaft), especially at low speeds.

Something of a scientific art is required to achieve just the desired burning pattern from the injected fuel. The injectors spray fuel into the cylinder as one or more streams of tiny particles. As each of these particles encounters the superheated air of the cylinder, a chemical reaction begins between the outermost molecules in the particle and oxygen molecules in the air—the fuel particle starts to burn. In order for it to continue to burn, however, it must come in contact with additional oxygen molecules, and continue to do so until the reaction is complete.

Since only one of five molecules in air is an oxygen molecule, the chances of any fuel molecule meeting an oxygen molecule are initially just 20%. As the burning process continues, and the oxygen in the cylinder is steadily consumed, the chance of a fuel molecule encountering an oxygen molecule decreases. Injectors spray fuel in straight lines, and as a consequence, the farther the

fuel from the injector, the less the penetration of the air and the fewer available oxygen molecules will be encountered (see Figure 3-1).

Because of these factors, diesel engines are always designed to draw in more air than is strictly required to burn the amount of fuel injected. In this way complete combustion is assured, but the extra air represents underutilized engine capacity. More efficient combustion burns more of the available oxygen, which means greater power output from any given cylinder size.

Many different designs are employed in the attempt to use as much as possible of the

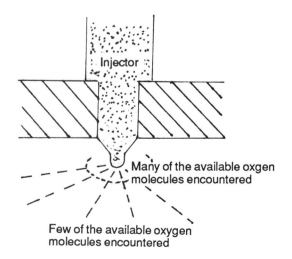

Injector

Many of the available oxgen molecules encountered

Few of the available oxygen molecules encountered

Figure 3-1. *Oxygen utilization.*

available oxygen, but for the most part, two types of variations exist:

1. the nature of the pattern formed by the fuel particles when they are sprayed into the cylinder (covered in the next chapter);
2. the shape and characteristics of the combustion chamber into which the fuel is sprayed (the combustion chamber being that cylinder volume left when the piston is at the top of its compression stroke).

The spray pattern and combustion chamber are designed so that in combination they create a great deal of turbulence in the air within the cylinder. This turbulence widely disperses the fuel particles, so that the available oxygen mixes with the fuel as completely as possible.

The most common types of combustion chamber are: open or direct chamber; precombustion chamber; swirl chamber; and air cells.

The *open combustion chamber* is the simplest. It consists of a space left at the top of the cylinder when the piston is at the top of its stroke, or a hollow in the crown of the piston, or a hollow in the cylinder head, or a combination of these. Relatively little air turbulence is created in the cylinder, so an open combustion chamber is frequently combined with a *high-swirl* piston crown that is shaped to create air turbulence (see Figure 3-2).

An open combustion chamber has three principal advantages over other types:

1. Its simplicity.
2. The surface area of the combustion chamber relative to its volume is low. This helps to prevent heat dissipation and results in high thermal efficiency. It also makes starting easier because less compression heat is lost to the cold engine. Compression ratios are generally lower on open-combustion-chamber engines (around 16:1 as opposed to 20:1 in other types of diesels). This in turn leads to less stress on the engine.
3. The air is not forced in and out of ancillary chambers, as is the case in all other types of combustion chambers (this is often described as *work being done on the air*). As a result, an open combustion chamber creates fewer friction losses than any other variation, which leads to higher mechanical efficiency.

An open combustion chamber, however, generally has the lowest utilization of available oxygen of any type of chamber, and engines equipped with open chambers produce less power for a given cylinder size than do other types of diesel engines.

A *precombustion chamber* has a separate chamber cast in the cylinder head, its volume being between 25% and 40% of the total combustion chamber volume. The fuel is injected into this chamber, begins to burn, and is then forced by rising temperature and pressure through an orifice into the main

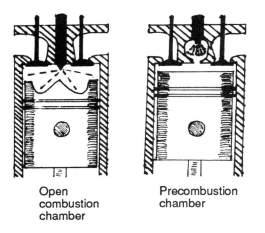

Open
combustion
chamber

Precombustion
chamber

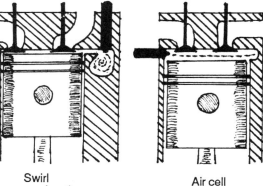

Swirl
combustion
chamber

Air cell

Figure 3-2. *Types of combustion chamber.*

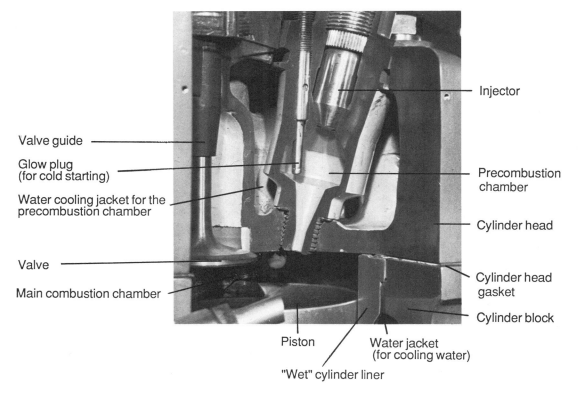

Figure 3-3. *Cutaway view of an engine with a precombustion chamber. (Courtesy Caterpillar Tractor Co.)*

chamber, creating a high degree of turbulence and air penetration in the process.

A precombustion chamber uses available oxygen at a greater rate, but thermal efficiency decreases because of increased heat losses through the greater surface area of the two combustion chambers. These engines can be difficult to start when they are cold, so compression ratios are generally high (20:1), and glow plugs are almost invariably installed in the precombustion chamber to aid in cold starting. Forcing the air and gases in and out of the precombustion chamber also causes more friction losses.

Swirl combustion chambers contain almost the entire compression volume of the engine set off in a chamber to one side of the cylinder. As the compressed air is forced into

it, it sets up a swirling motion. The diesel is then injected into this swirling mass. Air utilization is high, but a relatively large amount of work is done on the air, leading to higher friction losses than in other combustion chambers.

An *air cell* is an open chamber opposite the injector. Fuel is sprayed across the piston into the air cell, and combustion takes place throughout.

The main purpose in describing different chambers has been to give an overall feel for the combustion process; this helps when troubleshooting. Also, the next time a glossy engine advertising brochure pushes the merits of a ''high-swirl combustion engine,'' you will know just what is being described.

Chapter Four

Fuel Injection

Two of the requirements of a fuel injection system are to break up the injected fuel into minute particles (this is known as *atomization*), and to distribute these particles as thoroughly as possible around the combustion chamber.

The fuel injection system must also inject a precisely measured quantity of fuel at an exact moment and at a suitable rate of flow. Advances in these three areas created the greatest breakthroughs in the development of diesel engines.

Consider a four-cylinder, 4-cycle engine running at 2,000 r.p.m. and burning two gallons of diesel an hour. Each cylinder is being injected every two revolutions; with four cylinders there are two injections per revolution—4,000 injections per minute, 240,000 injections per hour. At two gallons of fuel per hour, the volume of fuel admitted at each injection is:

$$2/240,000 = 0.0000083 \text{ gal.}$$
$$(8.3 \text{ millionths of a gallon}).$$

At the same time, the fuel must be raised to a pressure of 1,500 to 5,000 psi (depending on the system) to overcome the pressure in the cylinder and ensure proper injection.

Not only must the fuel system precisely measure out this minute quantity of fuel at these high pressures, but it must do so equally from revolution to revolution and from cylinder to cylinder so that all bear an even load.

At 2,000 r.p.m. the crankshaft completes 33⅓ revolutions per second. Each piston travels up and down 66⅔ times per second, and the *total time* of the power stroke is thus 1/66.66 second or 0.015 second. During this instant, the fuel system must initiate the fuel injection, control it at a particular rate, and cut if off. To do this effectively the beginning point of the injection must be timed to an accuracy of 0.0015 second or better.

The rate of injection is extremely important. If the fuel is pushed in too fast, combustion accelerates and creates excessive temperature and pressure, high loads on the engine, and uneven running. If the fuel comes in too slowly, a portion of it is still burning as the piston is well on its way down on the power stroke; this fuel contributes little power to the engine and will cause a smoky exhaust.

These facts and figures serve only to illustrate that a *diesel engine fuel system is an incredibly precise piece of engineering and needs to be treated with a great deal of respect.* The injector and injection pump are two pieces of equipment that an amateur should generally leave alone, but understanding how they function may help diagnose a problem.

There are three different fuel injection systems in common use on small diesel engines: jerk pumps, distributor pumps, and common rail units.

Jerk pumps. Jerk pumps consist of a

plunger moving up and down in a barrel, actuated by a camshaft mechanically driven off the engine. Each injector has its own pump, although on small engines with more than one cylinder all the pumps are normally housed in a common block and driven by a common camshaft (these are known as *in-line* pumps). On large engines individual pumps are normally fitted to each cylinder.

Jerk pumps work as follows: When the plunger is at the bottom of its stroke, an inlet port in the barrel is uncovered and fuel under low pressure from the feed or lift pump is admitted. The plunger is then driven up the barrel, forcing the fuel through a *delivery* valve and then to the attached injector. The plunger has a curved groove machined in it, which at a specific moment lines up with a *spill-off* port in the barrel, allowing the fuel pressure to be bled off and end-

ing injection for that stroke. By rotating the plunger or barrel, the groove and spill-off port can be lined up at different points on the plunger stroke, thus regulating the amount of fuel pumped. This is the function of the engine throttle, which is linked to the plungers or barrels.

Each time a pump strokes, it sends a shot of high-pressure diesel to its injector, forcing open a valve in the injector and spraying into the cylinder. A small amount of fuel is allowed to leak past the valve stem and spring in the injector in order to lubricate everything, and is returned to the fuel tank via a *leak-off* or return pipe from the injector. Figure 4-1 shows the workings of a typical jerk pump, and Figure 4-2 shows the arrangement of the pump plungers and barrels.

Distributor pumps. Distributor pumps

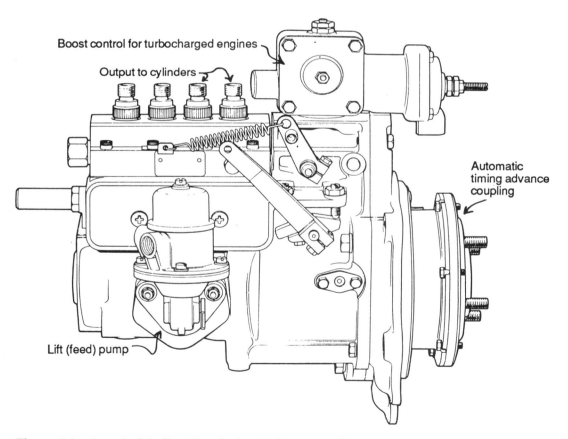

Figure 4-1. *A typical in-line (4 cylinder) jerk pump. (Courtesy Lucas CAV Ltd.)*

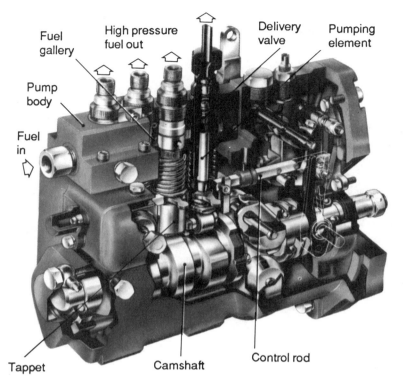

Figure 4-2. *Arrangement of plungers and barrels in an in-line, jerk-type fuel injection pump. (Courtesy Lucas CAV Ltd.)*

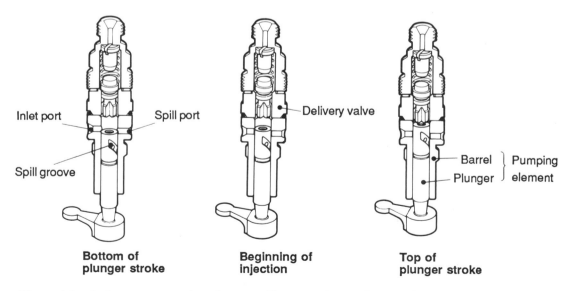

Figure 4-3. *Jerk pump pumping element. (Courtesy Lucas CAV Ltd.)*

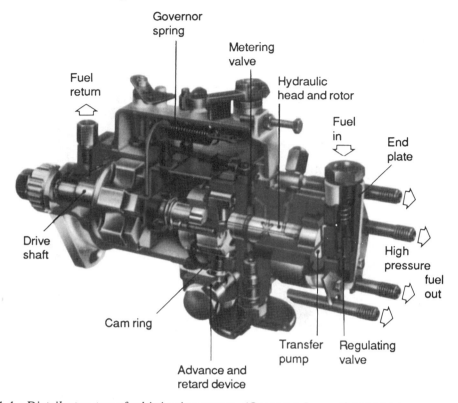

Governor
spring

Metering
valve

Hydraulic
head and rotor

Fuel
return

Fuel
in

End
plate

Drive
shaft

High
pressure
fuel
out

Cam ring

Transfer
pump

Regulating
valve

Advance and
retard device

Figure 4-4. *Distributor-type fuel injection pump. (Courtesy Lucas CAV Ltd.)*

employ one central pump with a rotating device that lines up the output with each cylinder's injector in turn, much as the distributor on a gasoline engine sends the spark to each spark plug in turn. The operation is then the same as a jerk-pump system. Distributor pumps are far more compact than jerk pumps. Because the same pump feeds all cylinders, every injector is guaranteed an equal amount of fuel, ensuring even engine loading and smoother running at idle speeds. A metering valve on the inlet port to the pump barrel regulates the volume of fuel entering the pump, which controls engine speed. Figure 4-4 shows a distributor pump. Figure 4-5 shows a typical distributor pump fuel system.

Modified (or low pressure) common rail units. These use a pump of much lower pressure than the other two systems. Fuel circulates constantly through a common supply pipe to all the injectors, each of which contains its own high-pressure pump and is actuated directly by an engine-driven cam. The supply pipe (or rail) has a pressure-relief valve that maintains a constant pressure and permits excess fuel to flow back continuously to the fuel tank. The common-rail system is in widespread use on General Motors 2-cycle diesels, but few of these turn up in pleasure boat use. The overwhelming majority of small-boat diesel engines use either a multiple jerk pump or a distributor pump.

From an injection pump the fuel passes to an injector (Figure 4-6), which contains a needle valve held by a spring against a seat in the tip of a nozzle. When the pump raises the pressure of the fuel in the injector, the needle valve lifts off its seat and fuel sprays through the tip of the nozzle into the cylinder.

Injectors are generally classified by the type of nozzle they employ—either *hole-type* or *pintle* (Figure 4-7). Hole-type nozzles

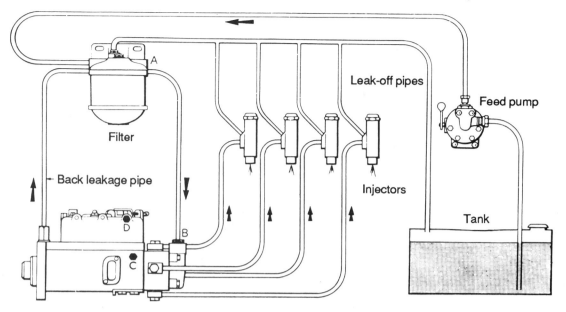

Figure 4-5. *Typical fuel system with distributor pump. (Courtesy Lucas CAV Ltd.)*

have one or more tiny holes in the tip through which the fuel is driven. By varying the size, number, and angle of the holes, varying degrees of fuel atomization, dispersal, and injection direction can be established.

Pintle nozzles have a central hole with a plunger (pintle) sticking through it. When in-

jection occurs, fuel sprays down around the sides of the pintle and into the cylinder in a conical pattern. By varying the shape and angle of the pintle, a variety of spray patterns can be formed.

Hole-type nozzles are frequently used on engines equipped with open combustion chambers. By decreasing the size of the

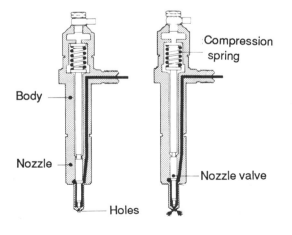

Figure 4-6. *Fuel injectors. Fuel entering the injector passes through galleries in the body and nozzle to a chamber surrounding the nozzle valve. The valve is held tightly closed by the valve spring until, on the fuel injection stroke, fuel pressure almost instantaneously rises above the preset spring pressure. The valve then lifts, permitting the high pressure fuel to pass through the hole(s) and spray the nozzle tip. At the end of the injection, the fuel pressure rapidly falls, the spring returns the valve to its seat, and the fuel injection spray into the combustion chamber is rapidly terminated. (Courtesy Lucas CAV Ltd.)*

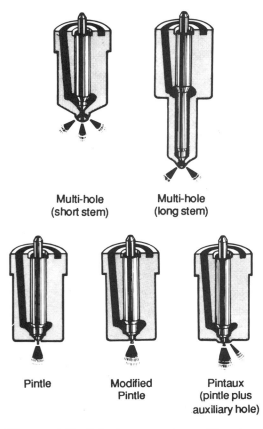

Multi-hole
(short stem)

Multi-hole
(long stem)

Pintle

Modified
Pintle

Pintaux
(pintle plus
auxiliary hole)

Figure 4-7. *Injector nozzles. (Courtesy Lucas CAV Ltd.)*

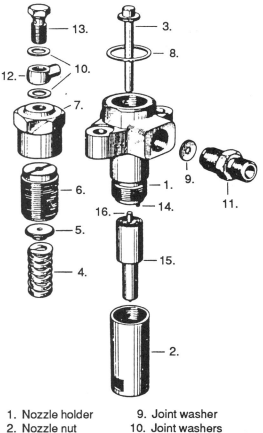

1. Nozzle holder
2. Nozzle nut
3. Spindle
4. Spring
5. Upper spring plate
6. Spring cap nut
7. Cap nut
8. Joint washer
9. Joint washer
10. Joint washers
11. Inlet adaptor
12. Leak-off connection
13. Banjo screw
14. Dowel
15. Nozzle
16. Needle valve

Figure 4-8. *Exploded view of a multi-hole injector. (Courtesy Lucas CAV Ltd.)*

holes, a greater degree of atomization of the fuel can be achieved. This assists the combustion process and helps to offset the poor air turbulence encountered in this type of combustion chamber.

Pintle nozzles are frequently used with precombustion chambers, the conical spray pattern ensuring a good distribution of the fuel throughout the chamber. There is less atomization of the fuel than in many hole-type nozzles, but once the initial combustion occurs and the expanding gases in the precombustion chamber carry the fuel particles out into the main chamber, a great deal of turbulence is created.

From the point of view of a maintenance-conscious boat owner, pintle nozzles have one distinct advantage: they tend to be self-cleaning through the action of the fuel washing down the sides of the pintle, whereas the extremely small holes needed in hole nozzles are more prone to clogging.

Chapter Five

Governors

The output of a gasoline engine is controlled by opening and closing a restriction known as a butterfly valve in the air inlet to the carburetor. The more the valve is opened, the more air enters the engine (picking up gasoline on the way) and the more power the engine puts out.

A diesel engine has no carburetor and no butterfly valve (with the exception of one or two older engines). The absence of any restriction in the air inlet is yet another reason why a diesel is more efficient than a gasoline engine, especially at low speeds and loads. (The lower the load and speed the more the butterfly valve is closed on the gasoline engine, and therefore the greater the pumping losses.)

The output of a diesel engine is controlled by regulating the amount of fuel injected into the cylinders. The pistons pull in about the same amount of air at each inlet stroke, regardless of engine speed or load. At low speeds and loads, very little fuel is injected, and the available oxygen is only partially burned up. As load and speed increase, more fuel is injected, until at full load enough fuel is injected to burn up all the available oxygen. This is the maximum power output that can be obtained from an engine. In practice, the maximum fuel injection is generally kept to a level at which only 70% to 80% of the available oxygen is burned, in order to ensure complete combustion and keep down harmful exhaust emissions.

In marine uses, one normally wants to be able to set the engine to run at a certain speed regardless of the load placed on it. This cannot be done by simply pegging the throttle at a certain point because every time the load increased or decreased, the engine would slow down or speed up. Constant-speed running is achieved by connecting the fuel-control lever on the injection pump to a *governor*.

The most basic type of governor consists of two steel weights, known as *flyweights*, attached to the ends of two hinged, spring-loaded arms, as in Figure 5-1. The governor's drive shaft is mechanically driven by the engine, and as it spins, the flyweights spin with it, pushed outward by centrifugal force. A *speeder spring* counterbalances the centrifugal force. Let us assume that the engine is running, the governor is spinning, and the flyweights are in equilibrium with the speeder spring at a certain position. If the load decreases and the engine speeds up, the governor spins faster and the flyweights move out under the increased centrifugal force. In moving out, their arms push up against the control sleeve, which compresses the speeder spring until sufficient counterbalancing pressure restores equilibrium. The control sleeve is connected by a series of rods to the injection pump fuel-control lever, and when the sleeve moves up the governor drive shaft it cuts down the injection pump's rate of delivery. The reduction in fuel slows the

23

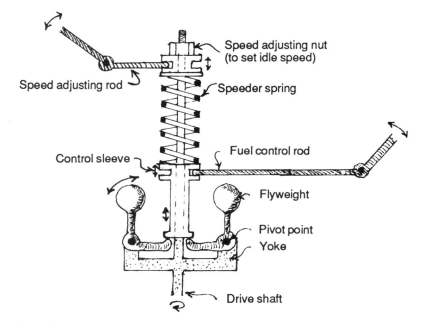

Figure 5-1. *A basic governor.*

engine down to the speed at which it was originally set.

If the load increases and the engine slows down, the centrifugal force on the flyweights decreases, and they move inward under the pressure of the speeder spring. In moving inward the flyweight arms allow the speeder spring to push the control sleeve down the drive shaft. This in turn operates the injection pump fuel-control lever, causing more fuel to be injected, which brings the engine back to its preset speed.

The engine can be set to run at any speed by adjusting the tension on the speeder spring via the speed adjusting rod. The greater the pressure on the spring, the more the flyweights will be held in, the more fuel will be injected, and the faster the engine will run. The less the pressure on the speeder spring, the easier it is for the flyweights to move out and the sooner the fuel injection rate will be reduced, allowing the engine to run at slower speeds.

All kinds of sophistications are built into many governors, and on larger engines the simple mechanical governor just described is replaced by a complex hydraulic one. The

principles are the same, but there is a qualitative increase in complexity. Some small marine diesels have the governor installed in the engine block, but there is an increasing tendency to build them into the back of the fuel injection pump. It is an item that rarely malfunctions. Beyond the occasional need to adjust the tension of the speeder spring in order to set up the engine idle speed, you should not need to know any more about governors than the information given here.

Vacuum-type governors

You may occasionally run across a vacuum governor. They operate as follows: A butterfly valve is installed in the engine air intake and a vacuum line hooked up from the air inlet manifold to a housing on the back of the injection pump. Inside this housing is a diaphragm that is connected to the injection pump's fuel-control lever, or *rack*.

The engine throttle operates the butterfly valve. When the throttle is shut down, the butterfly valve closes off the air inlet to the engine. The pumping effect of the engine pistons attempting to draw in air then pulls a partial vacuum in the air-inlet manifold, and this vacuum is transmitted to the housing on the fuel injection pump via the vacuum line and sucks the diaphragm in against a spring. The diaphragm pulls the injection pump control lever to the closed position.

When the throttle is opened, the butterfly valve opens, the manifold vacuum declines, the diaphragm moves back under the spring pressure, the fuel control rack increases the fuel supply, and the engine speeds up.

Aside from leaks in the vacuum line and around the diaphragm housing or a ruptured diaphragm (which are dealt with in Chapter 12) virtually nothing goes wrong with this system. The engine idle speed is set with the screw that adjusts the minimum closed position of the butterfly valve.

Chapter Six

Cooling

Diesel engines generate a great deal of heat, only one-third of which is converted to useful work. Of the remaining two-thirds, approximately half goes out the exhaust, and the other half has to be removed by the cooling system to prevent the build-up of damagingly high temperatures. Just to give some idea of the factors an engine designer has to take into account, consider the cylinder wall's temperature.

During combustion, temperatures in the cylinder rise to as high as 1,800 to 2,000 °F. If the cylinder wall is allowed to rise above 300 °F the engine oil will start to evaporate, the piston will lose its essential film of lubricating oil, and seizure will follow. On the other hand, one of the byproducts of combustion in a diesel engine is a considerable quantity of water. If the temperature of the cylinder wall remains too cool, this water will condense on the cylinder walls instead of vaporizing and exiting the engine with the exhaust gases. Water on the cylinder walls will:

1. wash away the film of lubricating oil from the cylinder walls;
2. find its way into the engine oil sump and cause emulsification and sludging of the oil;
3. react with various chemicals that build up in the oil to form corrosive acids, which attack the metal in bearings.

Maintaining the correct temperatures within an engine is important. In marine diesels, three principal methods are used:

1. *Raw-water cooling*—the sea, lake, or river water in which the boat floats is directly circulated through the engine to cool it and then passed back overboard.

2. *Heat exchangers*—the engine is cooled by an enclosed system, just as in an automobile, and the water in this system is then cooled by passing it through a *heat exchanger*. The heat exchanger consists of a cylinder with many small tubes running through it. The engine cooling water passes through the cylinder, whereas raw water is pumped through the small tubes, carrying off the heat of the cooling water. The raw water is then passed overboard. The heat exchanger performs the function of a radiator in a car, except that raw water, instead of air flow, dissipates engine heat.

3. *Keel cooler*—a variation on a heat exchanger in which, instead of bringing raw water into the boat, the heat exchanger is set *outside the boat* in the raw water, usually by running a pipe around the outside of the keel. The engine cooling water passes through this pipe and heat is dissipated directly to the water in which the boat floats.

Let us look at these three cooling systems in more detail.

Raw-water cooling

The principal advantage of raw-water cooling is its simplicity, which reduces engine

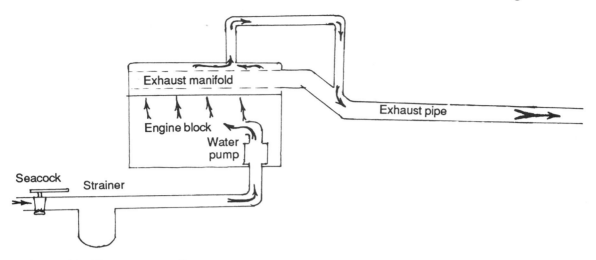

Figure 6-1. *Raw-water cooling.*

costs. The system has no heat exchanger and none of the associated pipework. Raw-water cooling, however, has a considerable number of drawbacks.

1. Although the raw water invariably passes through a strainer before entering the engine, small amounts of trash and dirt in suspension do find their way in. Silt picked up in muddy rivers tends to build up in pockets in the cylinder block and head, reducing cooling efficiency.

2. It is difficult to regulate engine temperature—first because the temperature of the raw water may range from the freezing point in northern climates in the winter to 90°F in tropical climates in the summer, and second because the inevitable bits of trash and silt could clog a thermostat, which is therefore usually omitted from raw-water-cooled engines.

3. In salt water, scale (or salt) tends to build up in the hottest parts of the cooling system, notably around the cylinder walls. This leads to a reduction in cooling efficiency. The rate of scale formation is related to the temperature of the water and accelerates when coolant temperatures are above 160°F. As a consequence, raw-water-cooled engines are generally kept at lower temperatures (normally around 140°F) than engines with closed cooling systems. This, in turn, causes water to condense in the cylin-

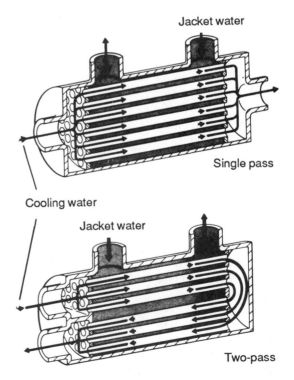

Figure 6-2. *Heat exchangers. (Courtesy Caterpillar Tractor Co.)*

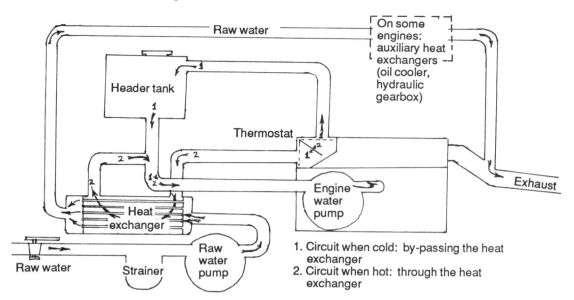

Figure 6-3. *Heat exchanger schematic.*

ders. What is more, these lower operating temperatures reduce the overall thermal efficiency of an engine. At the current state of technology, diesels are best run at temperatures around 185 °F, although this may rise in years to come with improved cooling techniques.

4. The combination of salt water, heat, and dissimilar metals is a potent one for electrolysis. Therefore, raw-water-cooled engines must be made of compatible materials: the primary choice is cast-iron cylinder blocks and heads, as opposed to the aluminum heads of high-speed, lightweight diesels. It is also essential to install sacrificial zinc anodes in raw-water-cooled engines.

Most raw-water-cooled engines are relatively slow-turning, heavy, cool-running, and unsophisticated but extremely long-lived and reliable. The vast majority of today's highly bred, lightweight diesels are cooled by heat exchangers.

Heat exchangers

A heat exchanger adds considerable expense, complexity, and weight to an engine, and it requires the addition of an extra pump (one

to circulate the engine cooling water, the other to circulate the raw water through the heat exchanger), but the system has several advantages.

1. The engine cooling circuit can be kept free of silt.

2. Engine temperatures can be closely regulated by a thermostat, which enables higher temperatures to be safely maintained.

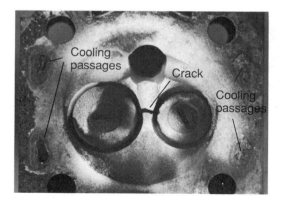

Figure 6-4. *Cracked cylinder head from a raw-water-cooled engine. The cooling passages were badly corroded from failure to change the sacrificial zinc anode. The engine then overheated and cracked the cylinder head.*

the pressure of water is raised, so too is its boiling point. If the pressure is raised by 10 psi, its boiling point increases to approximately 240 °F. By allowing the pressure to rise in a closed cooling system, overall higher system temperatures can be maintained with complete safety and without the risk of localized boiling at hot spots, which would create harmful pockets of steam.

4. Antifreeze and corrosion inhibitors can be added to the engine coolant, cutting out electrolysis and removing the risk of inadvertent freeze-up. The raw-water side of the heat exchanger, however, cannot be protected in this fashion; it is essential to use materials compatible with the marine environment and to protect them against electrolysis and freeze-up as necessary.

Side of block
split out

Figure 6-5. *Cracked block on a raw-water-cooled engine. This engine—mounted below the waterline with no siphon breaks—froze and split the block. When it thawed out, water flowed in through the cracked block and sank the boat!*

This promotes greater overall thermal efficiency and also lessens the risks of condensation occurring in the cylinders. Higher engine temperatures lead to a lowering of the viscosity or "thinning" of the engine oil, which reduces internal engine friction.

3. The closed engine-cooling circuit has an expansion tank with a pressurized cap, such as on an autombile's radiator. When

Keel coolers

The major advantage of a keel cooler is that no raw-water system is in the boat. This cuts out a fair amount of equipment (heat exchanger and raw-water pumps) and so keeps down costs. It also considerably reduces problems with electrolysis and eliminates the potential for frost damage in a raw-water circuit.

The major disadvantages of a keel cooler are the vulnerability to damage of the external piping; the need for extra holes in the hull below the waterline where the keel cooler enters and exits; and the additional drag caused by the keel cooler. No raw-water circuit within the boat means that no water is injected into the engine exhaust to cool and silence it (see next chapter).

In the long run, a properly maintained freshwater cooling system, either with a heat exchanger or a keel cooler, promotes engine efficiency and is likely to extend the life of an engine.

Chapter Seven

Exhausts

The exhaust is the other principal means of removing unused heat from the engine. Removing the spent gases from the cylinders after combustion, with as little resistance as possible, is just as important for effective combustion as refilling the cylinders with fresh air.

Any build-up of pressure in the exhaust system, known as *back pressure*, will rapidly reduce the overall efficiency of the engine. The power required to remove the exhaust gases from the engine is another component of the pumping losses mentioned in Chapter 2.

The exhaust gases of a 4-cycle engine are in part pushed out by the piston on its fourth stroke. High exhaust back pressure will not, therefore, prevent the removal of the exhaust gases, but it will cause the engine to work harder, run hotter, and lose power. The exhaust gases of a 2-cycle engine, however, are cleaned out by the pressure of the scavenging air being blown into the cylinders. A high enough exhaust back pressure will completely stall out this flow, and the engine will simply not run at all.

In order to improve gas flow through the exhaust system, most 2-cycle diesel engines have two exhaust valves per cylinder, instead of one. (Remember that a 2-cycle has no inlet valves—the incoming air enters through the ports at the base of the cylinder.) These exhaust valves open more suddenly than those of 4-cycle engines, so that evacuation of the cylinder can get underway as rapidly as possible. This causes much sharper pressure changes than in 4-cycle engine exhausts, which leads to considerably noisier operation. Only so much can be done to reduce 2-cycle exhaust racket, since the effectiveness of a muffler is dependent to a certain extent on the amount of back pressure that can be induced in the system.

The exhaust of a 4-cycle engine fitted with a turbocharger passes through a turbine as soon as possible after it exits the cylinders. The restriction caused by the turbine creates a certain amount of back pressure at this point. Once the gases have passed through the turbine, pressure in the rest of the exhaust must be kept to a minimum—any rise in back pressure at this point will seriously impair the turbine's efficiency.

The need to keep exhaust back pressure to a minimum leads to a couple of obvious requirements for an exhaust system:
1. The exhaust piping should contain as few bends as possible.
2. The piping must be of a large enough diameter to produce as little friction to the flow of gases as possible. The longer the exhaust pipe, the larger its diameter should be.

The least possible back pressure would be created by a short pipe going straight overboard, but the noise would be completely unacceptable and the pipe would be dangerously hot. Three approaches are usually taken to cooling and silencing the exhaust:

1. In raw-water-cooled engines, after coming out of the water jacket around the exhaust manifold, the engine cooling water is sprayed into the exhaust pipe and mixes with the exhaust gases (Figure 6-1). As the water is sprayed into the pipe, much of it evaporates, rapidly cooling the gases. This sharp reduction in temperature produces a corresponding fall in pressure, which reduces the back pressure in the system and slows down the exiting gases. The reductions in pressure and speed have a considerable silencing effect.

In engines fitted with turbochargers, the cooling water can only be injected into the exhaust system *after* the turbocharger. This is because the water would damage the turbine, but even if this were not so, the reduction in exhaust gas volume and speed caused by the fall in temperature when the water is sprayed in would considerably reduce the effectiveness of the turbocharger.

2. In engines with heat exchangers, the used raw water is sometimes injected into the exhaust system. The effects are as described above for raw-water systems (see Figure 6-3).

3. Sometimes no water is injected into the exhausts of raw-water-cooled or heat-exchanger-cooled engines, and this is always the case with keel coolers. The exhaust is cooled only by the water jacket around the exhaust manifold. Such an engine is said to have a *dry* exhaust. The exhaust pipes on these engines invariably run hotter than water-cooled exhausts and must therefore be appropriately insulated.

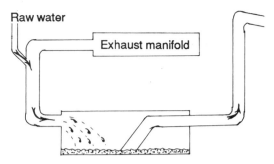

Figure 7-1. *Water-cooled and silenced exhaust.*

A dry exhaust has to be silenced with the familiar automobile-type muffler. A wet exhaust, however, can use the injected water for very effective silencing. Figure 7-1 illustrates how this is done.

The injected water builds up in the base of the muffler until it blocks the outlet pipe. At this point the back pressure starts to climb until it is high enough to blow the water out of the exhaust pipe. The small amount of pressure created has a tremendous silencing effect. The key thing, especially on turbocharged engines, is to keep the distance the water has to be lifted as short as possible—the higher the lift, the greater the back pressure.

Although wet exhausts are very effective and increasingly popular, several precautions regarding their installation must be observed, or water may find its way into the engine and do serious damage. These precautions are covered fully in Chapter 14, "Engine Installations."

Chapter Eight

Cleanliness is Next to Godliness

If a diesel engine has clean air, clean fuel, clean oil, and is kept clean, it will run for years without giving any trouble. If this book does no more than provide an understanding of why cleanliness is so important and instill in the reader the determination to change air, fuel, and oil filters at the specified maintenance intervals, it will have been a success.

Clean air

A diesel engine needs close to 1,500 cubic feet of air at 60 °F to burn one gallon of fuel. In Chapter 5 it was pointed out that only at full load is the entire air intake used for combustion; engine manufacturers design their engines to pull in 25% to 30% more air than the minimum required at full load, in order to guarantee that all the fuel in the combustion chamber burns. At anything less than full load, only a small percentage of air drawn into the engine is used in combustion, and the actual volume of air drawn in by a diesel engine per gallon of fuel burned is several times greater than the 1,500 cubic feet needed. Even a small, naturally aspirated engine can easily consume *every hour* more air than you'd need to fill a 20-foot by 20-foot room (see Figure 8-1). Turbocharged

engines use approximately twice as much air as naturally aspirated engines, 2-cycle engines, four times as much.

Every hour, day after day, sometimes year after year, a small diesel engine sucks in enough air to fill a large room, and yet as little as two tablespoons of dust contained in that air can do enough damage to necessitate a major overhaul.

The marine environment is relatively free of airborne pollutants; nevertheless, I hope you never again fail to check the air filter at the specified maintenance interval!

Air filters on small diesels are almost all of the replaceable paper-element type found in automobiles (see Figure 8-2), although one or two are the oil-bath type (Figure 8-3). In the latter, the air is forced to make a rapid change of direction over a reservoir of oil, and particles of dirt are thrown out by centrifugal force and trapped in the oil. The air then passes through a fine screen, which depends on an oil mist drawn up from the reservoir to keep it lubricated and effective. In time, although the oil looks the same, the reservoir fills with dirt, the oil becomes more viscous, less oil mist is drawn up, and the filter efficiency slowly declines. You must change the oil in the reservoir at the correct intervals.

The large volume of air used by a diesel

The volume of air required by a naturally aspirated 4-cycle engine running at 83% volumetric efficiency.							
CID*/liters	Engine speed (RPM)						Cubic feet per minute
	500	1000	1500	2000	2500	3000	
50/0.8	6	12	18	24	30	36	
75/1.25	9	18	27	36	45	54	
100/1.6	12	24	36	48	60	72	
125/2.0	15	30	45	60	75	90	
150/2.5	18	36	54	72	90	108	

*CID = Cubic Inches of Displacement

These figures are calculated with the following formula: $\dfrac{\text{CID} \times (^1/_2 \text{ engine speed}) \times 0.83}{12 \times 12 \times 12}$

Figure 8-1. *Air consumption table.*

engine emphasizes another requirement for efficient running—a well-ventilated engine room. All too often the engine is tucked away somewhere out of sight and out of mind, and in order to keep down noise and unpleasant smells, it is sealed up in a nice tidy box. That engine needs room to breathe if the box is not to be a coffin!

Clean fuel

A fuel injection pump is an incredibly precise piece of equipment. The plungers in a jerk pump are machined to within 0.00004″ of the cylinder bores into which they fit. Unlike the pistons in the engine, no rings seal these plungers, and while the pressures in the engine cylinders may reach 1,000 psi, pressures in an injection pump are anywhere from 1,500 to 5,000 psi.

The phenomenally accurate fit of the pump plungers in their cylinders is the only thing that prevents fuel from leaking past these plungers under extreme pressures. When you realize that the pump may be metering out only a few millionths of a gallon, you begin to understand how little leakage past the plungers it would take to completely destroy the smooth running and balance of the engine. If just one or two

Figure 8-2. *Air filter with replaceable paper element. (Courtesy Caterpillar Tractor Co.)*

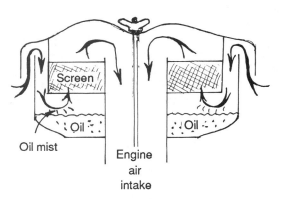

Figure 8-3. *An oil bath–type air cleaner.*

plungers are leaking by, then the other cylinders pick up more load, which leads to higher temperatures, excessive wear of exhaust valves, and the danger of cracking the cylinder head or seizing a piston.

Imagine a tiny grain of sand or a little speck of metal finding its way into the pump. Even if this contamination passes through the pump without scratching the cylinder or piston, or doing any other kind of damage, it will now be on its way to an injector. Depending on engine size and type of injector nozzle (hole-type or pintle) the holes in the tip of the nozzle through which the fuel sprays into the combustion chamber may be no more than a few thousandths of an inch in diameter. It takes the merest piece of trash to plug up an injector.

Water can be just as harmful to a fuel injection system. When the engine is shut down for periods of time, as is the norm for most boat engines, rusting of critical parts will occur, which rapidly destroys the effectiveness of the system. When the engine is running, the superheated air in the cylinders under compression will instantly turn into steam a tiny drop of water in the tip of an injector. This steam can generate enough explosive force to blow the tip clean off the injector.

Nothing plays more havoc with small-boat diesel engines than dirty fuel. CAV, one of the world's largest manufacturers of diesel injection equipment, estimates, "If right from the start the owner gets rid of dirt and water in the fuel, then 90% of potential engine troubles will be avoided." The damage done by dirty fuel is concentrated on all the most highly machined and therefore expensive pieces of equipment in the engine. Damage to fuel injection pumps and injectors cannot be repaired by the user.

The fuel system is the one area that should remain strictly off limits to the amateur mechanic, except in dire emergencies. With just a little vigilance, the fuel system will most likely never give any trouble, but just a few moments of carelessness or a little inattention to the filters can cause thousands of dollars of damage in no time at all.

An engine is equipped with at least one fuel filter (nowadays normally of the spin-on type used for automobile oil filters). Both a primary and secondary filter are needed, however, and any engine having only one filter should be provided with another. The primary filter is mounted between the fuel tank and the lift pump (if fitted); the secondary filter is mounted after the lift pump and before the fuel injection pump.

Primary and secondary fuel filters do not have the same function. A primary filter is the engine's main line of defense against water and serious contamination of the fuel supply. It does not guard against the odd particle of dirt—that is the function of the secondary filter.

The primary filter must be installed *before* the lift pump, because when water in the fuel supply passes through the pump it breaks up into small droplets that are much harder to separate from the fuel. A primary filter needs to be of the *sedimenter* type specifically designed to separate water from fuel. Sedimenters are extremely simple, generally consisting of little more than a bowl and a deflector plate. The incoming fuel hits the deflector plate and flows around and under it to the filter outlet. Any water drops and large particles of dirt are precipitated out by gravity *(settling out)* and centrifugal force *(jetting out)*. Primary filters have either:

1. a see-through bowl with a drain so that any water contamination can be rapidly detected and removed; or
2. a drain petcock on the base so that a sample can be taken at regular intervals to ensure that no contamination is occurring.

All kinds of sophistication can be built into primary filters, notably:

1. an electronic device that detects when the water reaches a certain level and either sounds an alarm or shuts down the engine via a fuel supply solenoid valve (more on this later);
2. a float that closes off the fuel supply when the water in the filter reaches a certain level.

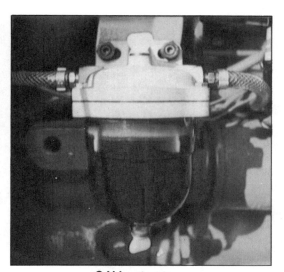

CAV watertrap

CAV waterstop

CAV waterscan

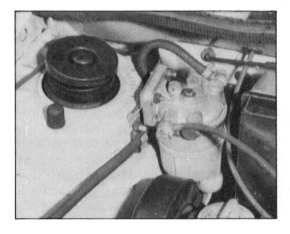

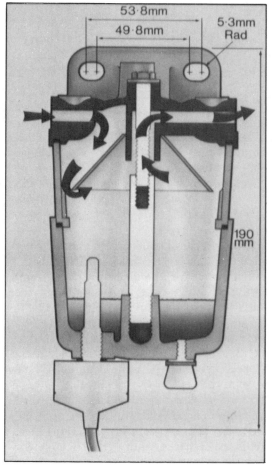

Figure 8-4. *Primary fuel filters. Fuel entering the CAV Waterscan passes over and
around the sedimenter cone, through the
narrow gap between the cone and the body,
and then to the center of the unit and out
through the head and outlet connections.
This radial flow causes water and heavy
abrasive particles to separate out by gravity
and collect in the bowl of the unit. There are
no moving parts. The electronic probe, fitted
in the base of the unit, contains two elec-
trodes. A third is provided by the fuel itself.
As the level of water increases, the balance
in the system is disturbed and a warning
signal provided. This signal can be used to
trigger a light, buzzer, or other device to
advise the operator of the need to drain the
unit. A simple thumb screw drain is provided. The system provides an automatic
circuit check that triggers the warning device
for a period of 2 to 4 seconds when the
system is first energized. (Courtesy Lucas
CAV Ltd.)*

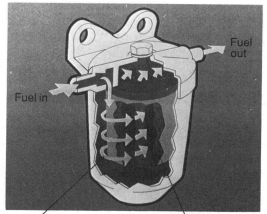

Swirling motion causes larger particles of dirt to be thrown out by centrifugal force

Replaceable paper element

Figure 8-5. *Primary fuel filter with 9 micron mesh. (This filter differs from the Lucas CAV filter in Figure 8-4 in that it has a paper element as well.) (Courtesy Caterpillar Tractor Co.)*

Regular draining of the filter bowl should be all that is needed. *If an engine does not have a primary filter of this type, the cost of installing one may seem high, but this cost will pale into insignificance compared to the cost of repairing damage from contaminated fuel.*

Secondary filters have a much finer screen to collect any small particles of dirt still suspended in the diesel fuel. A secondary filter is of no use as a primary filter—the fine screen will plug up too quickly, and it is not designed for water separation. *The correct type and mesh of filter has to be used in the right place.*

Secondary filters contain a replaceable paper filter element (a *strainer*) that is specified by its *micron* size, which is the size of the largest particle that will pass through the filter element. A secondary filter screen should be in the region of 7 to 10 microns (as opposed to a primary filter, which should be no finer than 10 microns and may well be as coarse as 25 microns). The better secondary filters also incorporate a drain and are known as *coalescers* or *agglomerators*. This

refers to their ability to trap small droplets of water still suspended in the fuel supply. As the element stops more droplets, the water coalesces, or agglomerates, until the drops become large enough to settle out in the base of the filter, from where they can be periodically drained. Figure 8-6 illustrates a secondary filter with agglomeration capability.

It cannot be emphasized strongly enough that every marine diesel engine without exception must have properly sized primary and secondary filters.

Certain other measures need to be taken to protect the fuel injection system.

1. All cans used for bringing fuel on board should be kept scrupulously clean and for that purpose alone.

2. All fuel taken on board should be passed through a funnel with a fine mesh screen. If you detect any signs of contamination, refueling must cease at once.

3. You must take regular samples from the lowest point of the fuel tank to check for contamination. If you can't get at a drain valve on the underside of a tank, find some means of pumping out a sample of fuel. At the first sign of contamination, drain the tank or pump down the fuel until not a trace of contamination remains. Any especially dirty batch of fuel should be completely discarded—it is not worth risking the engine for the sake of a tankful of fuel.

4. Even if all the fuel taken on board is perfectly clean and the tank is clean, *contamination can still occur.* Moisture in the air at the top of the tank will frequently condense, and in the humid marine environment this condensate will steadily build up in the bottom of the tank. Various algae and bacteria also can live and breed in diesel fuel. These will lead to slimy deposits on the filters and can progressively plug up the fuel system. *No matter how careful you are in taking on fuel, you still need to take occasional samples from the tank.*

5. Various proprietary diesel treatment additives on the market will kill any algae or fungus, reduce sludge formation, and provide some corrosion protection to the fuel system, but some (especially those contain-

CAV FS filter

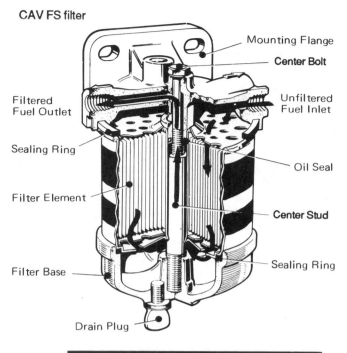

Mounting Flange

Center Bolt

Filtered
Fuel Outlet

Unfiltered
Fuel Inlet

Sealing Ring

Oil Seal

Filter Element

Center Stud

Filter Base

Sealing Ring

Drain Plug

Figure 8-6. *Secondary filter with "agglomeration" capability. (Courtesy Lucas CAV Ltd.)*

ing alcohol) will attack O rings and other nonmetallic parts in the fuel injection equipment. For this reason, as a general rule, most people who deal with fuel injection systems recommend against the use of any additives, except for ones designed strictly to deal with algae.

Techniques for changing fuel filters, which require that fuel lines be correctly bled, are covered in Chapter 9. For now, remember, *the fuel must be kept clean.*

Clean oil

The higher temperatures in diesel engines subject the lubricating oil to great stresses. The oil can break down into its basic compo-

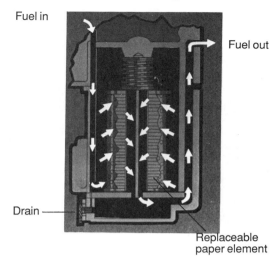

Fuel in

Fuel out

Drain

Replaceable
paper element

Figure 8-7. *Another style of secondary filter.
(Courtesy Caterpillar Tractor Co.)*

nents of hydrogen and carbon, which promotes the build-up of carbon deposits in the engine. Carbon deposits also come from improperly burned fuel that is scraped down into the crankcase by the piston rings. This accounts for the characteristic black color of diesel engine oil even after only a few hours of engine running time.

Carbon accumulates around cylinders and on pistons, piston rings, valves, and valve seats. Heat can bake it onto these surfaces, and if it's left unchecked, it will steadily build up and prevent valves and piston rings from seating properly, which causes *blow-by*. Compression is lost, rings wear, valves burn away, and cylinders become scored. Power is lost, and the engine runs hot. Starting becomes more and more difficult.

The breakdown of a diesel engine's lubricating oil also causes oxidation of various trace elements, principally sulfur, which then combine with moisture to form corrosive acids. These acids are especially harmful to the key metallic surfaces in all the major bearings. The moisture with which the trace elements combine is another by-product of combustion. For every gallon of diesel fuel that's burned, about one gallon of water vapor is formed. Some of that condenses on colder surfaces and finds its way into the oil sump.

To deal with these potentially harmful by-products, diesel engine oil is specially formulated. Detergents added to the oil hold the carbon in suspension and prevent it from building up on engine surfaces. Other additives take care of any acid build-up. *Using the correct oil in a diesel engine is vitally important. Many perfectly good oils designed for gasoline engines are not suitable for use in diesel engines.*

As the oil does its work, the detergents and additives are steadily used up. The oil wears out. It must be replaced at frequent intervals, far more frequently than in gasoline engines. Every time you change oil, you must install a new filter to rid the engine of all its contaminants.

Modern diesel engines run at higher speeds, higher temperatures, and higher pressures than many older diesels. The newer lightweight diesels have smaller oil reservoirs than older engines. The smaller amount of oil is therefore working much harder. *This considerably magnifies the importance of carrying out the oil changes at the specified intervals.*

If regular oil changes are not carried out, sooner or later the carbon will overwhelm the detergents in the oil and lead to the formation of a thick black sludge in the crankcase. Meanwhile, carbon will begin to build up on pistons, cylinders, and valves. Water and oxidized sulfur will combine to form sulfuric acid, which goes to work on the engine's principal bearing surfaces, and it will also start to emulsify the rest of the

Dirt	43%
Lack of oil	15%
Misassembly	13%
Misalignment	10%
Overloading	9%
Corrosion	5%
Other	5%
	100%

Figure 8-8. *Major causes of bearing failure.*

engine oil. The sludge will begin to plug some of the slower-moving oil passages, and may eventually cause a complete oil failure in parts of the engine. As is shown in Figure 8-8, 58% of all bearing failures are the result of dirty oil or lack of oil.

A clean engine

A clean engine is as much a psychological factor in reliable performance as a mechan-ical one. The owner who keeps the exterior clean is more likely to care about the interior. Maintenance is less onerous: Nothing will more likely make you put off an overdue oil change than the sight of a soot-blackened, dirty, greasy hunk of paint-chipped cast iron, with diesel fuel, old oil, and smelly bilge water slopping around in the engine drip pan.

Chapter Nine

Troubleshooting, Part One—Failure to Start

When I was working on oil platforms in the Gulf of Mexico, the most common emergency call I received went something like this: "Such and such engine won't start. It was working fine the last time I used it, but now it just won't run." I asked three questions before calling up a boat or helicopter to go and investigate:

1. "Have you checked to see if it has any fuel?"
2. "Have you checked to see if the fuel filter is plugged up?"
3. "Have you left any life in the battery?"

"Oh, sure," was the answer, and probably half the time I found the engine out of fuel, the filter plugged, the battery dead, or a combination of these. Fuel can easily be added, and a clean filter can be fitted, but you can't get around a dead battery.

If an engine does not start as usual, you should stop cranking and start thinking. That extra couple of cranks in the hope of some miracle never fails to guarantee that the engine cannot be started at all.

If an engine has air, adequate compression, and a correctly metered and timed charge of fuel, it more or less has to fire. So first check for these.

Air supply

Does the engine have air? A stupid question, you may think, but certain engines (notably GM 2-cycles) have an emergency shutdown device, a flap that completely closes off the air inlet to the engine and guarantees that no ignition will take place. I have on several occasions flown to a platform to investigate an engine that would not start only to find the air flap closed. (Note that stopping an engine by closing the air flap will soon damage supercharger air seals and should only be done in an emergency, such as engine *runaway*—more on this later.)

If the engine does not have an air flap, what about the air filter? It may be plugged, especially if the engine has been operated in a dusty environment. It may have a plastic bag stuck in it, or even a dead bird (which I found on one occasion). If the boat has been laid up all winter, a bird's nest may be in there. The point is, take nothing for granted. A problem with the air supply is unlikely, but you need only a few minutes to check it.

Compression

If you find no obstruction in the air supply, perhaps the air charge isn't being adequately compressed. Although numerous variables are at work here, you must attempt to isolate them in order to identify problems.

Cranking speed

Cranking speed is important for a number of reasons. The slower the engine turns over, the more time there is for air to leak past poorly fitting piston rings and badly seated valves, which reduces compression. The slower the cranking speed, the longer the air charge will be cooled by the cold metal surfaces of the engine. As a consequence, a higher degree of compression will be required to reach ignition temperatures. The slower the cranking speed, the slower the fuel pump operates, and the greater the tendency for injectors to dribble rather than produce a high-power penetrating spray. And the slower the cranking speed, the less the degree of turbulence imparted to the air charge and the poorer the mixing of the fuel and air. *Low cranking speeds are a guaranteed source of starting difficulties* (see Figure 9-1).

First check to see that the problem is not simply a result of leaving the engine in gear or the clutch activated on a refrigeration compressor or some other piece of auxiliary equipment. Assuming this is not the prob-lem, the most likely candidate is battery trouble.

A diesel engine must have an adequately charged heavy-duty battery reserved solely for starting the engine—the boat's electrical supply should come from another battery. The very high compression ratios of diesel engines impose much higher loads on the battery than do gasoline engines. Heavy-duty battery cables, well connected at both ends, will be needed to the starter motor. For a given size of wire, the longer it is, the greater the voltage drop, and therefore power loss, through it. This power loss can only be overcome by increasing the size, or gauge, of the wire. In order to keep the cable run as short as possible, you should mount the battery as close as you can to the starter motor, but proper marine installations require an isolation switch that permits completely removing the battery from the circuit in the event of an emergency such as an electrical fire.

Isolation switches are generally located in the boat's main electrical panel, which is frequently some distance from the battery and the starter motor. In this case, the only way to reduce power loss to a minimum is to use larger-than-normal wire sizes. Welding cable, available from welding-supply houses,

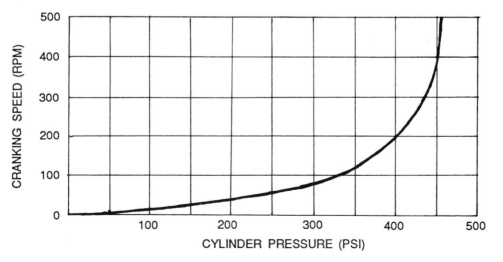

Figure 9-1. *Approximate relationship of engine cranking speed to cylinder pressure.*

is not an unreasonable choice for a battery cable.

If at any time a battery cable or terminal becomes warm to the touch, you may be fairly sure that the cable isn't big enough, that you have a poor connection, or both. If you experience difficulties with cranking and know that the battery is fully charged, remove the cables, clean the mating surfaces, and securely refasten. Be sure to include the ground cable—its connection to the engine block is frequently a source of trouble—because the electricity that flows from the battery through the positive cable must return through the negative side.

Exceptionally cold weather thickens the oil in the crankcase, which considerably increases the initial friction in the engine. If the engine is equipped with a decompression lever and a hand crank, turning it over a few times by hand may help break the oil's grip.

The battery's output is also adversely affected by cold. Assuming 100% cranking power at 80 °F, this falls to 65% at 32 °F and to 40% at 0 °F. In extreme cases, you may have to remove the engine oil and warm it, warm the water in the cooling system, and warm the battery in order to achieve an adequate cranking speed.

Cylinder lubrication

As an engine operates, the lubrication system maintains a fine film of oil on the cylinder walls and the sides of the pistons. This oil plays an important part in maintaining the seal of the piston rings on the cylinder walls. After an engine is shut down, the oil slowly drains back into the crankcase. An engine that's been shut down for a long period of time may suffer a considerable amount of blow-by when you try to start it for the first time, because the lack of oil on the cylinder walls and piston rings reduces the seal and, therefore, compression.

Open the throttle wide, crank the engine over for a few seconds, then let it sit for a minute. Very often some of the small amount of diesel fuel that sprayed into the cylinders will find its way onto the topmost piston ring and be just enough to bring the compression up to starting level when you crank the engine again. The heat of compression during the initial cranking will also have taken the chill off the engine, which will help raise the compression temperature. If this method fails, a small amount of oil introduced into the cylinders will sit on the piston rings and help raise compression.

Some engines have small oil caps installed on the air inlet manifolds for squirting oil into the cylinders. These are little tubes fitted to the topside of the manifold. A hinged lid covers each, and each has a small hole in the base that leads into the manifold. The cups are filled with oil from a squirt can, and the cranking action of the engine draws oil out of the cups into the cylinders.

The majority of engines do not have these oil cups, but you can achieve the same results by removing the air cleaner and squirting some oil into the air inlet where it will be drawn into the cylinders. Be careful of the amount of oil that you squirt in—oil isn't compressible, and if it fills the combustion chamber, damage to the piston and rings may occur.

Valve and piston blow-by

Blow-by caused by serious wear to the valves, piston rings, or cylinders will make engine starting increasingly hard. Here, you must determine which cylinder has the worn part and whether the valves or the pistons are at fault.

Inject some oil into each cylinder in turn, then crank the engine. If you notice a marked improvement in compression on any cylinder, that's the one suffering blow-by around the piston and rings. If compression does not improve, suspect the valves. A hand crank on the engine helps in performing these tests, because you can slowly turn the crankshaft and rock each piston against compression. As each piston comes up to compression, you will feel the crank handle try to bounce back. You should not be able to hand-crank a healthy engine at slow speeds without the use of decompression levers. If you can crank it through, suspect considerable blow-by. You can frequently tell whether the pistons or valves are the

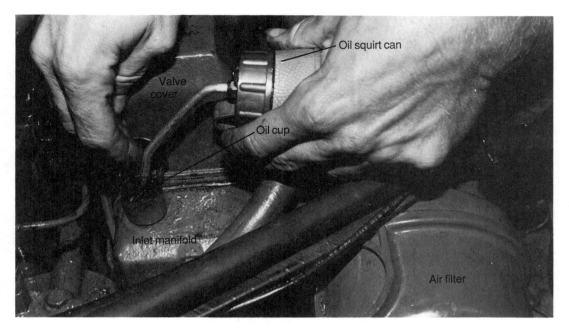

Figure 9-2. *Putting oil in an oil cup fitted to the air-inlet manifold of a Sabb 2JZ diesel engine.*

culprits by listening for the hiss of escaping air.

If engine compression is suspect, more precise determinations can be made using a compression tester, but this is a specialized piece of equipment that will require calling in a diesel mechanic.

Carbon build-up on a valve stem occasionally will cause that valve to stick in its guide in the open position. This should not happen if you follow proper oil change procedures, but should tests indicate valve blow-by, the valve cover (rocker cover) should be removed and the valve stems observed for correct operation. If work has recently been performed on the cylinder head or valves, it is also possible that one of the valve clearances has been incorrectly set (see Chapter 11), and the valve is being held in a permanently open position.

Miscellaneous

A loss of compression can be caused by a blown or leaking cylinder-head gasket, but unless the head has been recently removed, there is little reason to suspect this. The symptoms will resemble those of leaking valves, and because the head must be removed to sort out the valves, the gasket problem will become evident right away.

Engine wear, especially in the piston pin and rod end bearings, eventually may increase the cylinder-head clearance to the point at which adequate compression cannot be achieved. Little can be done to cure this, short of a major engine rebuild. Before this point is ever reached the engine will give advance warning by *knocking* pretty badly (see Chapter 10).

Finally, it is possible for the operator of an engine fitted with decompression levers to leave these levers in the decompressed position, which ensures that the cylinder has no compression at all—silly, but worth checking before taking more drastic action. If an engine is shut down by using the decompression levers instead of closing the fuel rack on the injection pump, serious damage is likely to occur to the valves and push rods. If you suspect that this might have occurred, the valve cover should be removed and the valves checked for bent stems or push rods.

Fuel supply

If the engine is cranking smartly and has adequate compression but still won't start, the culprit is almost certainly the fuel system. The fuel system has the potential for causing a considerable number of problems. Some are easy to check; others can only be guessed at.

Throttle

Diesel engines are shut down by closing off the fuel supply. While on some engines this occurs when the throttle is closed down, others are set to idle at minimum throttle, and a separate "stop" control is fitted to shut off the remaining fuel supply. The first thing to check on the latter kind of engine is that the stop control hasn't inadvertently been left pulled out. On either kind of engine, one should then check that the throttle is fully open (or in the position specified by the engine manufacturer) and that it is actually advancing the governor control lever on the engine if remote controls are fitted. (This lever can be found by following the throttle cable.)

Solenoid

Many newer engines have solenoid-operated fuel shutdown valves, these being held in the closed positions when the engine is off. When the ignition switch is turned on it energizes a magnet, which opens the valve. Anytime the electrical supply to the solenoid is interrupted, the magnet is de-energized and the spring closes the valve. Any failure in the electrical circuit to the valve will automatically shut off the fuel supply to the engine. Given the problems with electrical circuits in the marine environment, if the engine appears to be getting no fuel and has a solenoid valve, this should probably be the first thing checked.

Some solenoid fuel valves are fitted directly onto the fuel injection pumps. You can identify the solenoid by a couple of wires coming off the back of the pump close to the fuel inlet line. Others are mounted separately but close to the injection pump. A rod coming from the back of the valve actuates a

Figure 9-3. *Solenoid-operated fuel shutdown valve.*

lever on the pump. You can check the operation of a solenoid valve by connecting it directly to the battery with a jumper wire. Take care to get the positive and negative leads the right way around. If the valve has only one wire, that is the positive lead, and the ground will be made through the body of the valve and engine block.

Tank and filters

Check the tank to make sure it has fuel in it, and remember that the suction line is normally set an inch or two above the bottom of the tank so that water and sediment will not be drawn into the fuel line. The primary fuel filter often has a see-through bowl, and it should be checked for water and sedimentation; if the filter is opaque, the drain on its base should be opened and a sample taken.

It is not uncommon for the primary fuel filter to be completely plugged. If this is so, no chances should be taken. Both it and the secondary filter must be replaced. If there is no primary filter, or any sign of contamination getting through the primary filter, you'll find a screen inside diaphragm-type lift pumps; it may be plugged and will need to be checked if the engine has this kind of lift

Figure 9-4. *Fuel filter in a lift pump.*

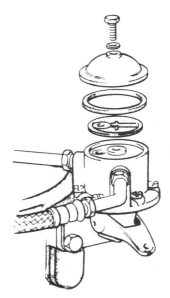

pump. You can reach it by undoing the center bolt and removing the cover. Assuming the filters are clean and the tank has fuel, the next step is to find out if there is air in the fuel lines.

Bleeding the fuel system

Air trapped in the fuel system can bring most diesels to a complete halt, although the extent to which this is so varies from engine to engine. On many older diesels with jerk pumps, even tiny amounts of air will stop the injection pumps from working, whereas many newer distributor pumps are capable of purging themselves to a considerable degree. When air does have to be purged by hand, the process is known as *bleeding the fuel system*.

Typical fuel systems are shown in Figure 9-6. The fuel is drawn from the tank by a lift pump (sometimes called a *feed pump*) and passes through the primary filter. The lift pump pushes it on, at low pressure, through the secondary filter to the injection pump. The injection pump meters it and pumps precise amounts of fuel at precise times, at pressures of anywhere from 1,500 to 5,000 psi. The fuel passes to the injectors and is sprayed into the cylinders. Any surplus fuel at the injectors is returned to the tank via *leak-off*, or return, pipes. (On some engines the lift pump is incorporated into the back of

To clean the gauze strainer in the lift pump

1. Remove the cover and joint from the top of the fuel lift pump and remove the gauze strainer.
2. Carefully wash any sediment from the lift pump.
3. Clean the gauze strainer, joint, and cover.
4. Reassemble the lift pump. Ensure that a good joint is made between the lift pump body and the cover because any leakage here will let air into the fuel system.

Figure 9-5. *Cleaning the lift pump. (Courtesy Perkins Engines Ltd.)*

the fuel injection pump rather than being a separate item.)

The more cylinders an engine has, the greater the number of fuel lines, and the suction lines, delivery lines, and injector lines added to the maze sometimes confuse the engine's owner. If that happens to you, remember that the secondary fuel filter is generally mounted on the engine close to the fuel injection pump, whereas the primary filter is generally mounted off the engine, or on the engine bed, closer to the fuel tank—you should have no trouble identifying those lines. The filters should have an arrow on them to indicate the direction of fuel flow;

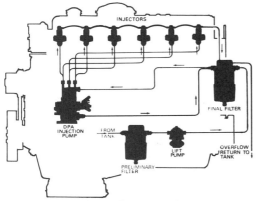

A: Distributor-type pump

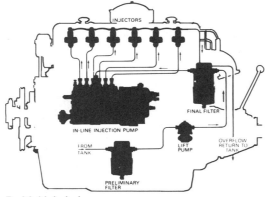

B: Multiple jerk pump

Figure 9-6. *Fuel system schematics. (Courtesy Lucas CAV Ltd.)*

sometimes the ports will be marked "in" and "out." Working from this and diagrams in the book, you should be able to construct a fuel-flow schematic and identify the fuel system components.

At various points in the system, you will find bleed-off nipples—normally on the filters and injection pump. One should be located on top of the secondary filter. On the base of the lift pump is normally a small handle, enabling it to be operated manually. This handle is pumped up and down. If it has little or no stroke, the engine has stopped with the lift pump drive cam at or near the full stroke position, and will have to be turned over half a turn or so to free the manual action. (See the section on lift pumps below for a more complete explanation of this.)

Figure 9-7. *Fuel lift pump (with supply line disconnected).*

Engines with no external lift pump generally have a manual pump attached to the injection pump, one of the filters, or at some other convenient point in the system. Bleeding follows the same procedure as with a lift pump.

Open the bleed nipple on the secondary filter and operate the lift pump. (If the filter has no bleed nipple, the fuel pipe connections can be loosened.) Fuel should flow out of the bleed nipple *free of all air bubbles.* If bubbles are present, you will have to operate

Figure 9-8. *Manual operation of a lift pump. (Courtesy Perkins Engines Ltd.)*

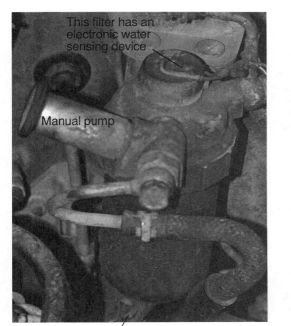

Figure 9-9. *Manual fuel pump on a filter.*

Figure 9-10. *Bleeding a secondary fuel filter. (Courtesy Perkins Engines Ltd.)*

the lift pump until they are clear. Then close the nipple. This should have purged air from the suction lines all the way back to the tank, including both filters. If any of the fuel lines have a hump or high spot, however, a bubble of air may well remain at this point and prove extremely hard to purge.

The next step is to bleed the fuel injection pump. Somewhere on the pump body you will normally find one, or perhaps two, bleed nipples (some of the modern pumps are self-bleeding and have no nipples). If the pump has more than one, open the low one first and operate the lift pump until fuel free of all air bubbles flows out. Close the nipple and repeat the procedure with the higher one. The injection pump is now bled.

The final step is to bleed the fuel lines from the injection pump to the injectors. To do this, set the governor control (throttle) *wide open* (this is essential), and crank the engine so that the injection pump can move the fuel up to the injectors. This should take no more than 30 seconds. In any event, a starter motor should never be cranked for

Figure 9-11. *Bleeding the fuel inlet pipe to a distributor-type fuel injection pump. (Courtesy Perkins Engines Ltd.)*

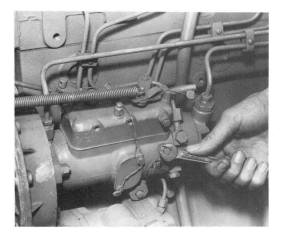

Figure 9-12. *Bleeding the lower nipple on a CAV DPA distributor-type fuel injection pump. (Courtesy Perkins Engines Ltd.)*

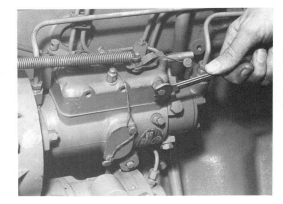

Figure 9-13. *Bleeding the upper nipple on a CAV DPA distributor-type fuel injection pump. (Courtesy Perkins Engines Ltd.)*

more than 30 seconds at a time, since serious damage can result through internal overheating. If the engine has decompression levers and a hand crank, turn it over by hand to avoid running down the battery.

If the engine has no hand crank, it is imperative that the system be properly bled to the injection pump before this last step is attempted. The battery is most often already low through earlier desperate cranking attempts, and pumping up the injectors one time, let alone having to come back and try again if re-bleeding is necessary, will be touch and go.

When the fuel eventually reaches the injectors, provided the engine is not running, you can hear the moment of injection as a distinct *creak*, and you can often also feel it as a *knock* in the appropriate fuel line. It is a good idea for a boat owner to become familiar with this noise and feel. For instance, if you can recognize the sound and it is present when you make the first unsuccessful attempt to crank the engine, then fuel is reaching the engine and you may dispense with the whole fuel bleeding process.

If you are unsure that fuel is getting through to the injectors, or if the injection pump is having trouble purging the lines of air, slacken an *injector nut*—it's the nut that holds the fuel line to the injector. If fuel is

getting through, a tiny dribble will be squeezed out of the slackened nut at every injection stroke of the pump for that cylinder. If no fuel comes out, you will have to turn over the engine until bubble-free fuel appears.

Do not overtighten the injector nut after you have completed the bleeding, because you may collapse the fitting that seals it to the injector. *Any time you have loosened an injector nut, you must check it for leaks while the engine is running. Fuel leaks on some engines may drain into the crankcase and dilute the lubrication oil, which can lead to engine seizure.*

Persistent air in the fuel supply

You may not be able to clear all of the air from the fuel system, or it may keep recurring. The source of the air must be found and the problem remedied. The most likely candidate is a poor connection somewhere between the fuel tank and the lift pump, because this is the only part of the system under suction pressure. A pinhole may have worn in a fuel line that has been rubbing against the engine or a bulkhead; the bleed nipple on the primary filter may not be tightly closed; if the primary filter has been changed recently, perhaps the filter housing was not snugged down and its rubber seal is allowing air to be sucked in; or maybe the

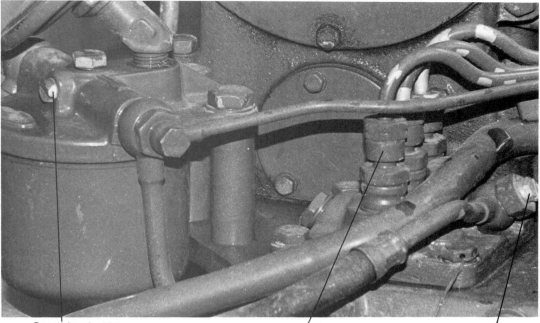

Secondary fuel filter
bleed nipple

Fuel lines to injectors

Fuel pump bleed nipple

Figure 9-14. *Bleed points on a Volvo MD 17C.*

fuel *is* lower than you thought, and should be checked again. If fuel sloshes around in the tank, it may allow little slugs of air to be sucked in.

Tracking down persistent sources of air can be aggravating. The only way to do it is to be methodical. Starting with the line from the primary filter to the lift pump, break it loose at the filter, place it in a jar of *clean* diesel, hold it below the level of the lift pump (this is important, or it will just set up a siphoning action), and operate the pump. If

Valve cover

Decompression lever (in decompressed position)

Injector hold-down nut

Injector leak-off pipe

Injector nut

Figure 9-15. *Injectors on a Volvo MD 17C.*

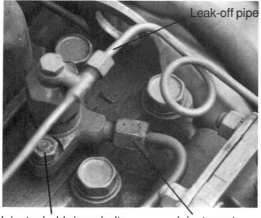

Leak-off pipe

Injector hold-down bolts   Injector nut

Figure 9-16. *Location of injector nut.*

fuel is drawn through free of air, replace that line and go to the next one back toward the tank. Repeat the procedure until you have isolated the offending line or seal.

The lift pump

The almost universal pump on engines fitted with separate lift pumps consists of a housing containing a suction and discharge valve and a diaphragm. A lever, which is moved up and down by a cam on the engine camshaft or crankshaft, pushes the diaphragm in and out. This lever can also be activated by a manual lever provided for that purpose, but if the engine has stopped in a position that leaves the diaphragm lever fully depressed, the manual lever will be ineffective until the engine is turned over far enough to move the cam out of contact with the lever.

A lift pump is a pretty foolproof piece of equipment, but occasionally the diaphragm will fail. Should no fuel be pumped when you manually operate the lever, the diaphragm may be holed. In this case, fuel is likely to be dripping out of a bleed hole in the base of the pump housing. (Recent Coast Guard regulations call for the elimination of this bleed hole.)

Occasionally you may run into another problem with lift pumps. In some sailboats with deep hulls and integral tanks (that is, built into the hull), the bottom of the fuel tank may be as much as three feet or more below the level of the engine-mounted lift pump. This may well exceed the rated lifting capacity of the pump. When the tank is low on fuel, the pump will lift too little fuel or none at all. Problems do not normally arise on starting, however, but manifest themselves as a loss of power under full load caused by fuel starvation at the injection pump.

On newer engines it is becoming increasingly common to dispense with an independent lift pump, and to incorporate it in the fuel injection pump. Two types are used:

1. On in-line jerk pumps, you'll find

Diaphragm cover screw

Diaphragm

Manual operation lever

Figure 9-17. *Diaphragm on a lift pump.*

Figure 9-18. *A gear-type lift pump (transfer pump). This pump is fitted to Caterpillar engines and performs the same function as a diaphragm lift pump (since there is no provision for hand pumping, a hand pump is incorporated on one of the fuel filters). Unlike a diaphragm pump, a gear pump will always put out more fuel than the engine requires. The excess is bled back to the inlet side of the pump or the fuel tank via a pressure relief valve built into the pump itself, or installed elsewhere in the fuel system. (Courtesy Caterpillar Tractor Co.)*

a piston-type pump in which a plunger is moved up and down by a cam on the same camshaft that operates the individual jerk pump plungers. These pumps generally incorporate an externally operated plunger for manual priming of the fuel system.

2. On distributor pumps, a rotary vane pump is driven off the central drive shaft. These pumps cannot be operated by hand; therefore, a separate manual pump is generally included in the system at some point, usually tacked onto one of the filters.

Very cold weather

The diesel fuel almost universally available in the United States is known as Number 2 diesel. At very low temperatures, it starts to congeal to the extent that it can plug up fuel filters and lines. If you suspect this is a problem, heating fuel lines and filters with a hair dryer or some other heat source may be all that is needed to get things moving. Number 2 diesel can be thinned with special low-temperature additives, kerosene, or Number 1 diesel if you anticipate prolonged extra-cold weather. Please note, however, that all of these decrease the fuel's lubricating qualitites, and running some engines on straight Number 1 diesel, for example, can lead to engine seizure.

Serious fuel supply problems

If the air supply is good, cranking speed is good, compression is good, the tank has fuel, and the system is properly bled, it is time to feel nervous and check the bank balance. Not too many possibilities remain —basically a worn fuel injection pump, worn or damaged injectors, or incorrect fuel injection timing.

There is just no reason for the injection timing to go out unless the engine has been stripped down and incorrectly reassembled. Only some serious mechanical failure is going to throw out the timing, in which case you should have had plenty of other indications of a major problem.

Worn or damaged injectors can lead to inadequate atomization of the injected fuel, to the extent that combustion fails to take place. Injectors are as precisely made as injection pumps and should only be disassembled as a last resort. Chapter 12 describes injector removal, cleaning, and checking procedures.

If the pump is so badly worn that proper injection is no longer occurring, you can do nothing except have it rebuilt or exchange it for a new one. Changing injection pumps is covered under the section on engine timing in Chapter 11.

Let me emphasize that these problems will almost never occur in a well-maintained engine. Just about every other fault should be suspected before them.

Exhaust

Starting problems, particularly on 2-cycle diesels, may occasionally be the result of excessive back pressure in the exhaust system. The most obvious cause would be a closed seacock. Other possibilities would be excessive carbon build-up in exhaust piping or a turbocharger. In cold weather there could even be frozen water in a water-lift-type muffler, which would have the same effect as a closed seacock.

Starting techniques

Let us assume that we have established that the fuel system is operating all right but we are having trouble achieving sufficient cranking speed or compression for one reason or another. One or more of the following suggestions may be all that is needed to do the trick.

1. The incoming air charge should be warmed as much as possible. Many engines already have some kind of cold-starting device fitted as standard equipment. The most common is a *glow plug*, a small electrical device installed in the combustion chamber that runs off the battery and becomes red hot. It ignites part of the incoming fuel charge, and the heat generated helps ignite the rest.

Less frequently, electric heating coils or *flame primers* are placed in the air-inlet manifold. These are similar to glow plugs, except that a small amount of fuel is ignited in the inlet manifold to warm the incoming air charge. Because a considerable amount of excess air is drawn into the engine at cranking and idle loads, the oxygen consumed by the flame primer does not prevent the engine from starting.

If these devices are not fitted or are out of order, their effect can be simulated in other ways. A hair dryer or other heat source can be used to warm the inlet manifold or incoming air, but caution must be used not to apply excessive heat to cold metal surfaces, or they may crack.

2. The engine should be warmed as much as possible, even to the extent of draining the engine oil and coolant, heating it, and replacing it. Once again, be careful— excessive temperature changes can lead to a cracked cylinder head or block. Warming the incoming fuel lines and filter with a hair dryer or other heat source will also help.

3. Oil squirted into the inlet manifold so that it will be drawn into the cylinders can raise compression considerably. Some engines have little oil cups fitted to the inlet manifold for this purpose. I prefer them to electrical devices because they are foolproof and draw no juice from the battery.

4. On an engine with decompression levers and hand cranking, the engine should be turned over a few times by hand to break the grip of the cold oil on the bearings. When cranking with the starter motor, the decompressors can be left in place until a good cranking speed has been attained, then closed.

5. If low cranking speeds are still a problem, you may have to disconnect auxiliary equipment, such as a refrigeration compressor or auxiliary pump, by temporarily removing the relevant drive belts.

6. *Starting fluid should not be used on diesel engines*. It is sucked in with the air charge, and being extremely volatile, will ignite before the piston is at the top of its compression stroke. This can result in serious damage to pistons and piston rods. Starting fluid has *no* place around diesel engines.

It is worth repeating that if you have any doubt about the engine starting, these measures should be taken *before* the first crank draws down the battery. It will take a lot less time to do this than it will to recharge the battery!

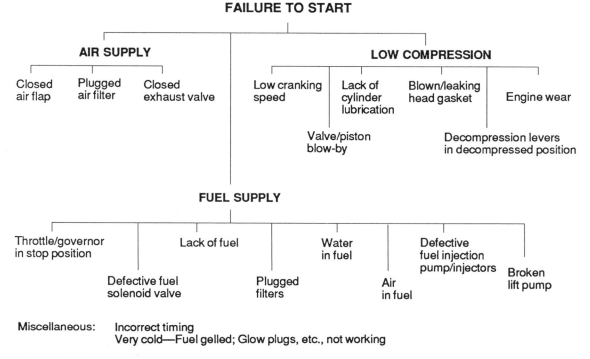

FAILURE TO START

AIR SUPPLY

Closed air flap

Plugged air filter

Closed exhaust valve

LOW COMPRESSION

Low cranking speed

Lack of cylinder lubrication

Blown/leaking head gasket

Engine wear

Valve/piston blow-by

Decompression levers in decompressed position

FUEL SUPPLY

Throttle/governor in stop position

Lack of fuel

Water in fuel

Defective fuel injection pump/injectors

Defective fuel solenoid valve

Plugged filters

Air in fuel

Broken lift pump

Miscellaneous: Incorrect timing
Very cold—Fuel gelled; Glow plugs, etc., not working

Figure 9-19. *Failure to start.*

Chapter Ten

Troubleshooting, Part Two

Knocks

Diesel engines make a variety of interesting noises. All the principal components create different sounds, and a good mechanic can often isolate a problem simply by detecting a specific *knock* coming out of the engine.

In addition to the injector creak already mentioned (Bleeding the fuel system, page 45), at any point on the valve cover you can hear the light tap, tap, tap of the rocker arms against the valve stems. (The adjusting screws used to set valve-lash clearance—see Chapter 11—are known as tappets.) With practice, anyone can pick up the note of individual tappets and get a pretty good idea if valve clearances are correct.

Crankshaft bearing noises can be picked up through the crankcase. They have a much lower *rumble*. A worn crank-end bearing on a connecting rod can be picked up as an audible knock. By testing different points of the crankcase and block, you can isolate the specific connecting rod at fault. (A good trick is to touch the tip of a long screwdriver to the engine while placing one's ear to the handle —it will act like a stethoscope, amplifying internal sounds. But be sure to keep clear of moving belts, flywheels, etc. . . !) Water

pumps, camshafts and fuel pumps each have their characteristic notes.

The symphony, however, is frequently garbled by a variety of fuel and ignition knocks. Differences in the rate of combustion can cause noises that are almost indistinguishable from mechanical knocks. But if the engine is run at full speed and then the governor control lever (throttle) shut down, closing off the fuel supply to the cylinders, a fuel knock will cease at once, whereas a mechanical knock will probably still be audible, albeit not as loudly as before because the engine is now merely coasting to a stop.

Some fuel knocks are quite normal, especially on initial start up. Remember that diesels are much noisier than gasoline engines, and have a characteristic clatter at idle, especially when they are cold. The owner of a diesel engine will have to become accustomed to these noises in order to detect and differentiate out-of-the-ordinary fuel knocks. These can have several causes.

1. Poor quality fuel (low cetane rating, dirt or water in the fuel): The fuel is slow to ignite and builds up in the cylinder. But then the heat generated by the early part of combustion causes the remaining (and now excessive) fuel to burn all at once. The sudden

Pressure diagram for an approximate 20:1 compression ratio, correctly timed with clean fuel and injector

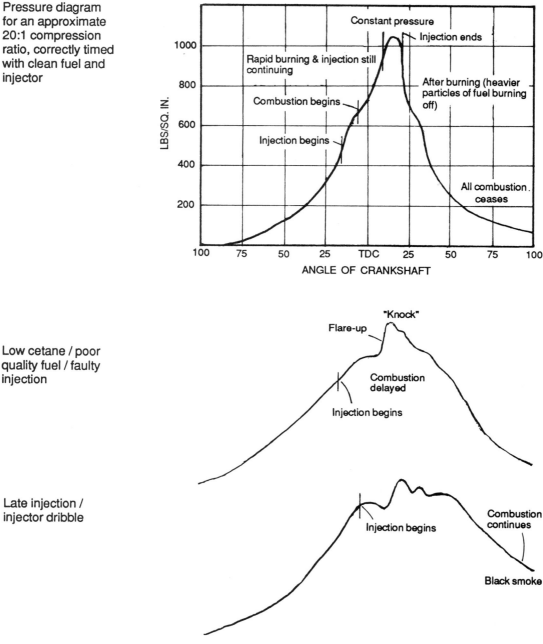

Low cetane / poor quality fuel / faulty injection

Late injection / injector dribble

Figure 10-1. *Fuel combustion pressure curves.*

expansion of the gases causes a shock wave to travel through the cylinder at the speed of sound. You will hear and feel this as a distinct knock (see Figure 10-1). It is known as *detonation*.

2. Faulty injection nozzles: These can produce a result similar to that just described. The fuel is not properly atomized and as a result, initial combustion is delayed. The fuel builds up in the cylinder and then a sudden flare-up occurs (see Figure 10-1).

3. Injection timing too early: This causes

the fuel to start burning while the piston is still traveling up on its compression stroke. The piston is severely stressed as the initial combustion attempts to force it back down its cylinder before the crankshaft has come over top dead center (TDC). Timing problems should not be encountered in normal circumstances.

4. Oil in the inlet manifold: On supercharged and turbocharged engines, leaking oil seals will sometimes allow oil into the inlet manifold. The oil is then sucked into the cylinders and can cause detonation. In extreme cases, enough oil can be drawn in to cause engine *runaway*; i.e., the engine speeds up out of control and will not shut down when the fuel rack is closed.

Runaway is more prevalent on 2-cycle engines than 4-cycle, and that's why 2-cycle engines have the emergency air flap that cuts off all air to the engine and strangles it. In the absence of an emergency air flap, the only way to stop a runaway is to cut off the oxygen supply, even by aiming a CO_2 fire extinguisher into the air inlet, although this will almost certainly damage the engine. Otherwise the runaway can continue until the supercharger/turbocharger oil supply is used up—and if this oil comes from the engine's oil supply, the engine will seize.

The more common mechanical knocks arise from:

1. Worn piston pin or connecting rod bearings. As the piston reaches top dead center (TDC) or bottom dead center (BDC), its momentum carries it one way while the crankshaft is moving in the other. Any play in the bearings will result in a distinct noise that varies with engine speed. A worn connecting rod bearing knocks louder under load.

2. Worn pistons will tend to *slap* or *rattle* in their cylinders. This is more audible at low loads and speeds, particularly when idling.

3. Sometimes valve stems will become coated with carbon and stick in their guides in the open position. When the piston comes up on its exhaust or compression stroke, it may well hit the open valve, knocking it shut or bending the valve stem and damaging the piston crown. In either event, you'll hear an unusual noise.

Sticking valve stems are generally a result of insufficiently frequent oil changes. As a temporary measure, they can often be relieved by lubricating the stem with kerosene and turning the valve in its guide to loosen it. At the earliest opportunity the cylinder head will have to be removed, and the valves, guides, etc., thoroughly decarbonized (see Chapter 11).

4. Worn main bearings *rumble* rather than knock. Engine vibration increases, especially at higher engine speeds.

Smoke

The exhaust of a diesel engine should normally be perfectly clear. The presence of smoke can often point to a problem in the making. The color of the smoke can be an even more useful guide.

Black smoke

Black smoke is the result of unburned particles of carbon from the fuel being blown out of the exhaust. This is likely to arise from overloading the engine, or from poor fuel injection.

If the engine is overloaded, the governor reacts by opening up the fuel-control lever until more fuel is being injected than can be burned with the available oxygen. This improperly burned fuel is emitted as black smoke.

Unfortunately, it is common practice to fit the most powerful propeller to a boat that the engine can handle in optimum conditions —meaning smooth water and with a clean, drag-free hull. In this way the performance of the boat under power is exaggerated, and overloading will result under normal operating conditions.

Apart from the likelihood of a smoky exhaust, overloading is liable to cause localized overheating in the cylinders, which could lead to an engine seizure and will definitely shorten engine life. Black smoke on new boats should always lead you to suspect engine overloading through the wrong propeller or too much auxiliary equipment. (Matching engines and propellers is dealt with in more detail in Chapter 15.)

If the fuel injectors have defective nozzles, causing improper atomization or a dribble after the main injection pulse, this will lead to unburned fuel and black smoke. If the engine is not overloaded, poor injection is the number-one suspect for black smoke. Other possibilities that should always be checked before tearing into the fuel system are:

1. Dirty air filter, causing insufficient air to reach the engine and resulting in unburned fuel.
2. A very high inlet air temperature, reducing the density (and thus the amount) of air entering the engine.
3. High exhaust back pressure, especially on turbocharged engines, causing the turbocharger to slow down with the same result as above—less air is pushed into the engine than it is designed for and fuel remains unburned, especially at high loads.

On many older engines any sudden attempt to accelerate will cause a cloud of black smoke as the fuel rack opens and the engine only slowly responds. Once the engine reaches the new speed setting, the governor eases off on the fuel rack and the smoke immediately ceases. This smoke is indicative of a general engine deterioration—the compression is most likely falling, the injectors need cleaning, and the air filter requires changing. If the engine is otherwise performing well, you have no immediate cause for concern, but the engine is serving notice that a thorough service is overdue. If smoking persists when the load eases off, the engine is crying out for immediate attention.

Blue smoke

Blue smoke arises from burning of engine oil. This oil can only find its way into the combustion chamber by making it up past the piston rings, or else down the valve guides and stems. In either case, decarbonizing is indicated (see Chapter 11). Unusual exceptions to this may be:

1. if pressure builds up in the crankcase, forcing oil up past the piston rings and into the combustion chamber, or if too much oil was added to the crankcase;
2. on turbocharged engines, if the oil seals on the turbine shaft leak into the inlet manifold, the oil will go directly into the combustion chamber.

White smoke

White smoke is caused either by water vapor, or totally unburned, but atomized, fuel. The former is symptomatic of dirty fuel, or possibly a leaking head gasket, cracked head, or cracked cylinder allowing water into the combustion chamber. The latter generally indicates that one or more cylinders are failing to fire. Air in the fuel sup-

SMOKE

Black	Blue	White
Lack of air:	Worn or stuck piston rings	Lack of compression
Dirty air filter	Worn valve guides	Water in fuel
Defective	Worn turbocharger /	Air in fuel
turbo / supercharger	supercharger oil seals	Defective injector
Overload	High crankcase oil level /	Cracked cylinder head /
Injector dribble	pressure	leaking head gasket
High exhaust back pressure		

Figure 10-2. *Smoke color and its causes.*

ply will, on occasion, cause misfiring with puffs of white smoke.

Misfiring cylinders

One or more misfiring cylinders will cause very rough running, and a simple procedure allows you to determine which cylinders are at fault. Start the engine, then loosen the injector nut at each injector in turn. The injector nut holds the fuel line to the injector. (In order to loosen these nuts, you may have to remove the valve cover for access on some engines.) Diesel fuel should spray out of the loosened nut, and the engine should slow or change its note, which indicates that this cylinder was firing but is now missing. Retighten that nut and loosen the next one. If diesel sprays out but there is no noticeable change in the engine, it is safe to assume that this cylinder is not firing. Of course, if no diesel sprays out, then you know why!

The primary cause of misfiring is low compression. A lack of fuel or poor injection will have the same effect. Sometimes a missing cylinder will pick up once the engine has warmed. This is generally evidence of low compression. As things warm up, the air charge in the cylinder reaches ignition temperature at the lowered compression level and the cylinder starts to fire. Erratic missing on all cylinders is a fair indication of either dirty fuel or a plugged air filter. If it is the former, corrective steps must be taken immediately before expensive damage occurs.

Overheating

Overheating can be the result of a number of things, but the primary suspect is always a blockage in the cooling system: a plugged up raw water filter, a blockage in the tubes in the heat exchanger, or silt and salt accumulation in the cooling passages and around the cylinder walls on raw-water-cooled engines. Perhaps someone forgot to open the cooling-water sea cock.

A water-cooled exhaust system should be set fairly high in the stern. Not only will this prevent following waves from driving up the exhaust pipe, it will also enable you to see at a glance whether the raw water side of the cooling system is functioning. It should be a matter of iron habit to check the exhaust for proper water flow every time you start the engine.

If you see an adequate flow of cooling water, you must look for other causes of overheating. In a proper engine and propeller installation, overloading should not be possible, but the addition of auxiliary equipment may change this. A rope wrapped around the propeller, or a heavily fouled hull bottom, will likewise greatly increase engine loading.

You must also look for mechanical causes. The water pump belt may be broken or slipping, or the pump itself may be defective (see Chapter 12 for more information on water pumps). Injection dribble can cause late burning of the fuel, which will heat up the cylinders at the end of the power stroke and would normally be accompanied by black smoke. This heat is not converted into work and must be removed by the cooling system. A low oil level may be causing partial seizure of one or more pistons, which will generate a tremendous amount of friction and heat on the cylinder walls.

Localized hot spots can cause pockets of steam to build up in cylinder blocks and heads. These can sometimes air-lock cooling passages, the cooling pump, the heat exchanger, or the expansion tank, especially if the piping runs have high spots where steam or air can gather. In certain instances if the raw-water intake is not set low enough in a hull, a well-heeled sailboat can suck in air and air-lock the raw-water pump. Alternatively, in an enclosed cooling system with a header tank, the water level in the tank may be too low.

Seizure

Seizure of the pistons in their cylinders is an ever-present possibility anytime serious overheating occurs, or the lubrication starts to break down. Overheated pistons expand excessively and begin to jam up in their cylinders. An engine experiencing seizure will begin to ''bog down''—that is, fail to carry the load, slow down progressively, probably emit black smoke, and become extremely hot. If steps are not taken to deal with the situation, total seizure—the engine grinding to a halt and locking up solidly—is, in all likelihood, not far off.

Partial seizure of individual pistons can occur as a result of uneven loading, causing overheating in the overloaded cylinder. Sometimes faulty fuel injection will cause the fuel to hit the cylinder wall and wash off the film of lubricating oil. Friction at this point will cause the piston to heat up and eventually seize. A late injector dribble can have the same result. I have even seen a new engine seized absolutely solid, while it was shut down, by the differential contraction of the pistons and cylinders in a spell of extremely cold weather.

If you detect the beginning of a partial engine seizure the correct response is not to shut it down immediately—as it cools the cylinders will lock up solidly on the pistons. The load should be instantly thrown off and the engine idled down as far as possible for a minute or so to give it a chance to cool off (this is assuming that the seizure is not due to the loss of the lubricating oil or cooling water—in either of these situations you have no choice but to shut down as fast as possible).

Poor pick up

Poor pick up, or failure to come to speed, is most likely the result of one or more of the following:

1. insufficient fuel caused by plugged filter or nearly empty tank;
2. dirty or clogged injector nozzles;
3. injection pump plungers leaking due to excessive wear;
4. clogged air filter;
5. excessive back pressure;
6. turbocharger malfunction;
7. low compression;
8. overloading;
9. too much friction—a partial engine seizure is under way.

High exhaust back pressure

High exhaust back pressure has been mentioned a number of times as a contributor to other problems. Its most likely causes are:

1. a closed or partially closed sea valve on the exit pipe;
2. carbon build up in the manifold, turbocharger (if fitted), or pipe;
3. too small an exhaust pipe, too many bends and elbows, or a kink in an exhaust hose.

The exhaust can reveal a surprising amount about the operation of an engine. One of the very best methods for monitoring the performance of an engine, used on all large diesels, is an exhaust pyrometer fitted to each cylinder. These measure the temperature of the exhaust gases as they emerge from the cylinders. Variations in temperatures from one cylinder to another show unequal work due to faulty injection, blow-by, etc., and should never exceed $\pm 20\,°F$. On occasion, exhaust pyrometers are offered as an option on smaller diesels, and for those inclined to do all their own troubleshooting and maintenance, these are a worthwhile investment. This is especially so with today's higher-revving, hotter-running, and more highly stressed engines. High exhaust temperatures on any cylinder will sharply decrease engine life. The additional cost of an exhaust pyrometer installation will easily be paid for in a better-balanced and longer-lived engine.

High crankcase pressure

Smoke blowing out of the crankcase breather or dipstick hole is an indication of high crankcase pressure. This condition is likely to develop slowly. It can be caused by excessive oil in the crankcase, but more likely is the result of poorly seating or broken piston rings, which allow the gases of combustion to blow by the pistons and into the crankcase. On turbocharged engines, the same result can occur if the oil seals begin to give out, allowing the turbocharger air pressure to blow down the oil drain lines into the crankcase.

Water in the crankcase

A certain amount of water can find its way into the crankcase from condensation of the steam formed during combustion, but appreciable quantities can only come out of the cooling system. The sources are strictly limited: a cracked cylinder head, a leaking cylinder-head gasket, a cracked cylinder liner (or one with a pinhole caused by corrosion from the water jacket side), or a leaking O ring seal at the base of a wet liner. All require the removal of the cylinder head and further close inspection.

You may encounter one condition, however, that is sometimes mistaken for a water leak. This is condensation in the valve cover, leading to emulsification of the oil in the valve cover, and rusting of the valve springs and other parts in the valve train. This will happen, from time to time, on an engine that the owner periodically cranks up for relatively short periods of time to charge a battery or just to make sure it is still working. In such a situation the engine never warms up properly, but enough heat is generated to create condensation in the valve cover. If an engine is started, it should be allowed to run long enough to thoroughly warm it up and drive all the moisture out of it. What is more, lightly loaded diesels run erratically (due to the difficulty of accurately metering the minute amounts of fuel required at each injection) and tend to carbon up. If at all possible, the boat should be firmly tied off, and the engine put in gear and given a bit of work to do. It will serve the twin purpose of warming it up faster and doing it some good.

Low oil pressure

Low oil pressure is a serious problem, but occurs infrequently. Many people confronted with low oil pressure assume that the gauge or oil warning light is malfunctioning and ignore the warning. Given the massive amount of damage that can be caused by running an engine with inadequate oil pressure, this is the height of foolishness. Any-

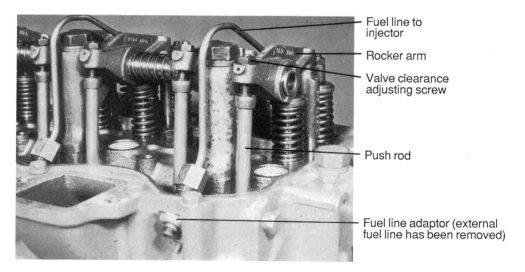

Figure 10-3. *Internal fuel lines. (This photo shows fuel lines inside a valve cover and their point of entry into the engine.) (Courtesy Caterpillar Tractor Co.)*

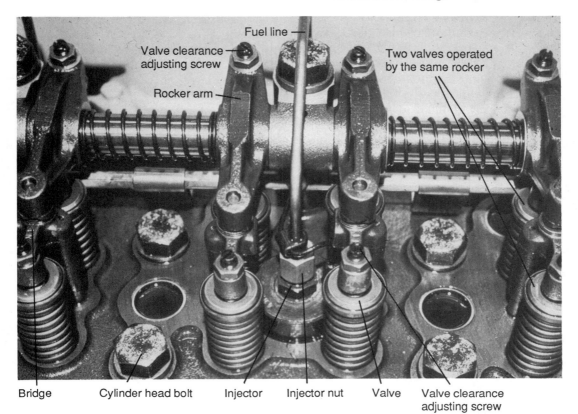

Figure 10-4. *Internal fuel lines. (This photo shows fuel lines inside a valve cover and the point of connection to the injectors. This high-performance engine has two exhaust and inlet valves per cylinder—the rocker arm operates a "bridge" which then actuates a pair of valves at the same time.) (Courtesy Caterpillar Tractor Co.)*

time low oil pressure is indicated, the engine should be shut down immediately and the cause discovered and rectified. The problem is likely to be one of the following.

1. Lack of oil. This is the most common cause of low oil pressure—and the least forgivable.

2. Dilution of the oil with diesel fuel. This will be shown by a rising oil level. Once enough diesel has found its way into the oil to lower the pressure to a noticeable extent, it will be possible to smell the fuel in the oil if you take a sample from the dipstick and rub it on your fingers. On some engines, all the fuel lines are external and diesel dilution of the oil is unlikely, but on many older engines

some fuel lines are internal and any fuel leaks will find their way into the crankcase.

3. The wrong grade of oil has been put in the engine. This may lead to the viscosity being too low. Another possibility is that overheating of the engine has caused a decrease in viscosity.

4. Worn bearings. The oil pump on an engine feeds oil under pressure through holes drilled in the crankcase (called galleries) and through various pipes to all of the engine bearings. Oil squeezes out between the two surfaces of the bearings and as the bearings wear, the oil flows out more freely with a resulting loss of pressure in the system. Worn bearings do not, as a rule, develop over-

night. A very gradual decline in oil pressure over a long period of time is likely to have taken place, with increasing engine noise and knocks. By the time a significant loss of oil pressure occurs, many other problems are likely to be evident, and a major rebuild is called for. Any rapid loss of oil pressure accompanied by a new engine knock indicates a specific bearing failure that needs immediate attention.

5. Oil pressure relief valve. When an engine first starts up, the oil is thick and cold. The oil pump can develop excessive oil pressure. On some engines the excess is vented directly back to the sump via a pressure relief valve. Should this valve malfunction due to a weak or broken spring, or trash stuck in the valve seat, it will cause the oil to bypass the engine and result in low pressure. Problems with pressure relief valves are rare but are simple to check. Almost invariably, the pressure relief valve is screwed into the side of the block somewhere and can be easily removed, disassembled, cleaned up and put back. The spring tension will need to be reset after this to maintain the manufacturer's specified oil pressure. Run the engine until it is warm and check the oil pressure. If it is low the engine should be shut down, the relief valve spring tightened a little, and the engine re-started. If no amount of screwing down on the pressure relief valve brings the oil pressure up to the manufacturer's specifications, the problem lies elsewhere.

6. The oil-pressure gauge. Oil-pressure gauges do occasionally malfunction but only rarely. The most reliable are the older mechanical ones (with an oil line connected from the engine block to the back of the gauge). Most modern engines have electronic sensing devices on the block (a *sender*) and electronic gauges. In the marine environment any electrical components are, in the long run, a liability, and these senders will sometimes go haywire. I am old-fashioned enough to prefer a mechanical gauge, but it should be noted that if the oil-sensing line ruptures (due to vibrations or whatever) it will spray engine oil all over the place.

7. The oil pump. Oil pumps rarely, if ever, give out as long as the oil is kept topped up and clean and the filter changed regularly. Over a long period of time, wear in the oil pump may produce a decline in pressure, but not before wear in the rest of the engine creates the need for a major rebuild. At this time the oil pump should always be checked.

8. If an engine has an oil cooler, the cooler can clog with sludge, restricting the flow of oil. This is likely to happen only if routine oil changes are seriously neglected, or the wrong oil (nondetergent) is used in the engine, in which case one had better look out for other problems!

Rising oil level

If the oil level in the crankcase starts to rise, it can only be due to water from the cooling system or diesel from a broken, leaking, or holed fuel line. In either case, it needs sorting out immediately.

Figure 10-5. Troubleshooting chart.

Seizure	Excessive oil consumption	Rising oil level	Low oil pressure	High exhaust back pressure	Loss of power	Overheating	Poor idle	Hunting	Misfiring	White smoke	Blue smoke	Black smoke	Knocks	Low cranking speed	Lack of fuel	Low compression	Poor starting	Cause
															X		X	Throttle closed
					X										X		X	Lift pump diaphragm holed
					X			X	X						X		X	Plugged fuel filters
					X			X	X				X		X		X	Air in fuel lines
															X		X	Empty fuel tank
					X			X	X			X	X				X	Dirty fuel
					X			X	X			X	X				X	Defective injectors
					X			X	X			X	X				X	Poor fuel quality
					X			X	X					X			X	Injection pump leaking by
					X			X	X			X	X				X	Injection timing advanced
						X						X						Too much fuel injected
	X				X		X		X	X						X	X	Piston blow-by
	X				X		X		X	X						X	X	Dry cylinder walls
					X		X	X	X	X						X	X	Valve blow-by
					X		X		X	X						X	X	Decompressor levers on
					X		X		X	X						X	X	Valve clearances wrong
					X		X		X	X						X	X	Valves sticking in guides
					X				X			X					X	Plugged air filter
				X	X							X					X	Plugged exhaust/turbocharger
				X	X												X	Kink in exhaust hose
X			X			X												Oil level low
X	X		X										X					Wrong viscosity oil
X		X	X															Diesel dilution of oil
			X															Dirt in oil pressure relief valve
			X															Defective pressure gauge
							X	X										Governor sticking/loose linkage
							X											Governor idle spring too slack
						X												Defective water pump
X						X												Defective pump valves
X						X												Air bound water lines
X						X												Closed sea cock
X				X		X												Plugged cooling system
X						X				X	X					X	X	Blown head gasket/cracked head
					X								X			X	X	Uneven load on cylinders
			X		X												X	Worn bearings
						X											X	Seized piston
				X										X			X	Auxiliary equipment engaged
														X			X	Battery low / loose connections
X						X	X					X						Engine overload / rope in prop.

63

Chapter Eleven

Overhauls, Part One— Decarbonizing

Sooner or later carbon buildup in the cylinders, on the pistons, and in the cylinder head will necessitate a decoke, a valve job and the removal of carbon deposits. In the case of engines whose valves are operated by push rods, this is well within the capability of an amateur mechanic and should give no cause for alarm. As in all other areas of maintenance, as long as the work area and engine are kept clean and the job is approached calmly and methodically you should encounter no insurmountable problems.

On engines with overhead camshafts (i.e., with the camshaft installed in the cylinder head, directly actuating the valves, therefore eliminating the need for push rods) removal of the cylinder head to carry out a decoke will disturb the valve (and possibly the injection pump) timing. At the end of this chapter the general principles that govern pump and valve timing are described, but a manufacturer's manual may be necessary to find out the specific procedure for timing any particular engine.

When should you carry out a decoke? There are two schools of thought: 1) to perform all maintenance at preset intervals, or 2) to wait until you have problems. The logic of the former position is that preset maintenance intervals will deal with conditions

likely to cause problems before they get out of hand. The logic of the latter position is that no two engines operate under the same conditions and one engine may run five times longer than another before it needs a decoke, or any other substantial overhaul. I lean toward the latter position.

"Leave well enough alone" is not such a bad idea, but you should be religious about routine maintenance, especially oil and filter changes and ensuring clean fuel. This alone will go a long way toward ensuring long intervals between substantial overhauls. Once a problem does begin to become evident (smoky exhaust, loss of power, difficult starting, etc.) you must rapidly deal with it. If these conditions are caused by valve or piston blow-by, for example, the hot gases will not take long to do some serious damage.

Decarbonizing consists of the removal of the cylinder head, and perhaps the pistons, and the removal of baked-on carbon from them and all their associated parts (valves, etc.).

Preparatory steps

The following must be done before the cylinder head can be removed.

Rocker arm (directly   Cam   Camshaft drive   Camshaft
actuated by camshaft)   sprocket   drive belt

Figure 11-1. *Overhead camshaft.*

1. The engine needs to be clean. Any time the engine is opened up, all kinds of damaging dirt will fall into it if it is not clean.

2. As a general rule, *everything that comes off an engine should go back on in the same place and the same way around.* This is especially important for moving parts (pistons, valves, push rods, rockers, etc.). All these parts wear where they rub on mating parts. If they are switched around on reassembly, a high spot on one part may now rub against a high spot on another part, and overall engine wear will greatly accelerate. Set aside a clear space and protect it with newspapers or a clean cloth. As parts come off the engine, spread them out in the correct relation to one another, and the right way around, so that you will not be confused on reassembly. Finding a suitable space on a boat is sometimes hard, but it should be done.

3. The engine must be drained of coolant to at least a level below the cylinder head. A drain valve or plug should be located somewhere at the base of the block. Since most sailboat engines are below the waterline, the engine-water seacock on a raw-water cooled engine must first be closed. On engines with heat exchangers and header tanks, the radiator cap on the header tank will need to be loosened to break the vacuum that will form when you drain the block.

4. All equipment attached to the cylinder head will have to be removed. This includes inlet and exhaust manifolds and turbochargers and intercoolers if fitted.

5. All injection lines will have to be broken loose from their respective injectors and the injection pump. *The minute any fuel line is disconnected, both it and the unit it is attached to must be capped to prevent the entry of ANY dirt into the fuel system.* The fuel lines should be numbered for ease of reassembly (a piece of masking tape and a felt-tip pen work fine). If the injectors are to be overhauled, it will be easier to get them out now, rather than when the cylinder head is off (see the section on injectors in Chapter 12).

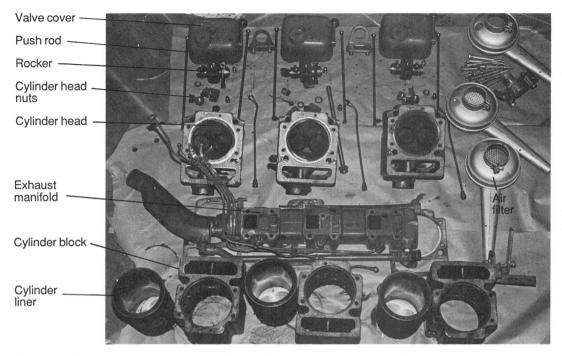

Valve cover
Push rod
Rocker
Cylinder head nuts
Cylinder head
Exhaust manifold
Cylinder block
Cylinder liner
Air filter

Figure 11-2. *Keeping things clean, tidy, and in the correct relationship to one another.*

Drains

Figure 11-3. *Cylinder block drains in a Volvo MD17C.*

6. Remove the valve cover and unbolt the rocker assembly. On some engines it comes off as one unit; on others each cylinder has a separate unit. The push rods (if fitted) can now be taken out and laid down in order (perhaps labeled, as with the injector lines).

7. On some engines with overhead camshafts, gears drive the camshaft but on others it is powered by a belt or chain. In

Exhaust manifold—an intermediary section of exhaust ducting has already been removed

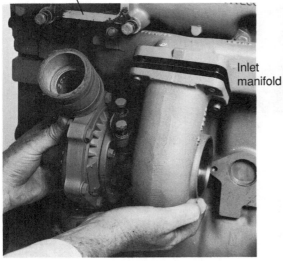

Inlet manifold

Figure 11-4. *Removing a turbocharger from the inlet and exhaust manifolds. (Courtesy Perkins Engines Ltd.)*

Injector hold-down nuts

Injector

Leak-off pipe

Injector pipe

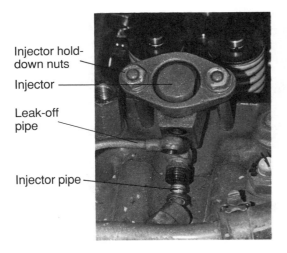

Figure 11-5. *Cylinder head with injector lines broken loose.*

Caps

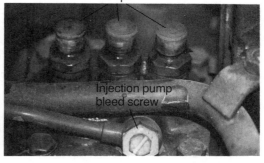

Injection pump bleed screw

Figure 11-6. *Fuel lines properly capped. (Volvo MD17C injection pump.)*

Oil supply to rockers

Cylinder head nut   Valve spring

Rocker arm

Figure 11-7. *Engine with valve cover removed.*

order to remove the rockers or the cylinder head, the belt or chain will first have to be taken off, which requires that the timing case cover on the front of the engine be removed. This generally calls for the removal of the crankshaft pulley, and more often than not this can only be done with a specialized tool, a gear or pulley puller.

If the pulley has any tapped (threaded) holes in its face, an improvised puller can be made. Slack off the pulley retaining nut. (The nut will probably have a lock washer with a tab that must first be bent back out of the way. The nut may be difficult to break loose, since the engine will turn over when pressure is applied. If a smart blow on the wrench fails to do the trick, place the engine in gear and lock it by putting a pipe wrench on the propeller shaft.) Next, bolt a flat metal plate, with a hole drilled in its

Figure 11-8. *Lifting off the rocker assembly. (Courtesy Perkins Engines Ltd.)*

Figure 11-9. *Cylinder head with rockers removed.*

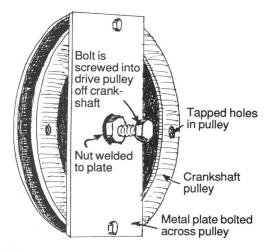

Figure 11-10. *A homemade crankshaft pulley puller.*

center and a nut welded over it, across the pulley, using the threaded holes in the face of the pulley. Screw a bolt down through the welded nut onto the end of the crankshaft, which will drive the pulley off the shaft (Figure 11-10).

Anytime you remove a timing belt or chain or a gear-driven camshaft, the fuel injection pump timing and the valve timing will be disturbed and will need resetting. This timing is absolutely critical to engine operation. If you have any doubt about

being able to reset either valve or injection pump timing, do not disturb them.

You are now ready to remove the cylinder head.

Cylinder head removal

The cylinder head is held down by numerous nuts or bolts spaced around each cylinder. In order to evenly relieve the pressure exerted on the cylinder head, loosen each nut a half-turn, or so, in the sequence outlined in the engine manual. If no manual is available, you should generally start with the nuts at one end, then the other end, and work into the center of the head. After you have released the initial tension, you can remove all the nuts.

A cylinder head will frequently bond to its cylinder block, making it difficult to break loose. When this happens, the temptation to stick a screwdriver in the joint between the two and beat on it with a hammer is dangerous and must be resisted. The tremendous pressures concentrated on the tip of the screwdriver can result in a cracked head or block. Instead, try turning the engine over; the compression will often be enough to loosen the cylinder head. Failing this, firmly hold a solid block of wood to the head at various points and give a moderate *whack* with a hammer or mallet. The shock should be enough to jar the head loose. The key to success is to ensure that the wood contacts a good area of the head; any point loading could crack the head. Be sure to give the wood a smart blow. If the head still refuses to budge, check to see that all the fastenings have been removed (it is surprisingly easy to miss one, especially on dirty engines).

When the head starts to come up, you must lift it clear squarely, in order to avoid bending the hold-down studs. Take care not to drag it across the top of the studs because you may scratch the face of the head.

The injectors of open-combustion-chamber (direct injection) engines protrude below the level of the cylinder head. Be careful not to rest the head on them or the nozzle tips will get damaged.

Anytime a head is removed, or any other piece of equipment, remember to block off all exposed passages and holes into the engine to prevent trash and engine parts from falling inside. It is unbelievably frustrating to drop a nut down an oil-drain passage and into the sump, and then be forced to remove the engine from the boat in order to drop the sump and recover the nut.

Once the head is off, both it and the face of the cylinder block will have to be cleaned of old gasket material and trash. Gaskets frequently become extremely well bonded to cylinder heads and blocks. Various proprietary scrapers can be bought from automotive stores, or an excellent scraper can be made from a length of industrial hacksaw blade (about 1″ wide and 6″ long) with one end ground into a chisel-like blade. In a

Figure 11-12. *A cylinder head removed (Volvo MD17C). Care must be taken not to rest the head on the injector nozzle. (Note that this is a direct combustion chamber engine; therefore there is no precombustion chamber in the cylinder head.)*

Figure 11-11. *Lifting off a cylinder head. (Courtesy Perkins Engines Ltd.)*

Figure 11-13. *A Volvo MD17C with cylinder heads removed. Note the "tor-oidal crown" pistons, since this is a direct combustion engine (see Chapter 3).*

pinch, try an old chisel (about 1″ wide) or any good-sized pocketknife. The key, especially on aluminum, is to keep the blade at a *shallow angle to the surface being cleaned*; otherwise one risks scratching or gouging the metal. Particularly stubborn residues require a great deal of patience.

With the head off, now is probably a good time to check it for warpage. Lay a straightedge (a steel ruler is excellent) across it at numerous points and attempt to slide a feeler gauge under it (see Figure 11-14). Feeler gauges are available from any automotive parts store. They consist of a number of thin metal blades, precision ground to the specified thickness stamped on the blade face. A set from 0.001″ to 0.025″—one thousandth of an inch to twenty-five thousandths—is needed, or the metric equivalent if you have a metric engine.

Allowable warpage varies according to cylinder head sizes. If the manufacturer's specifications are not available (as they almost certainly will not be) it is safe to assume that in the engine sizes under consideration here, any warpage over 0.004″–0.005″ (four to five thousandths of an inch) is excessive.

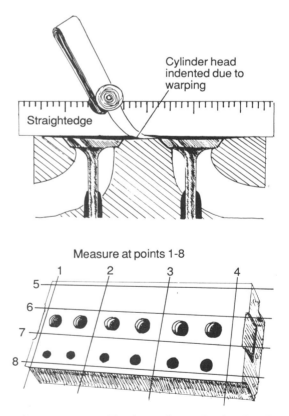

Figure 11-14. *Checking for cylinder head warpage.*

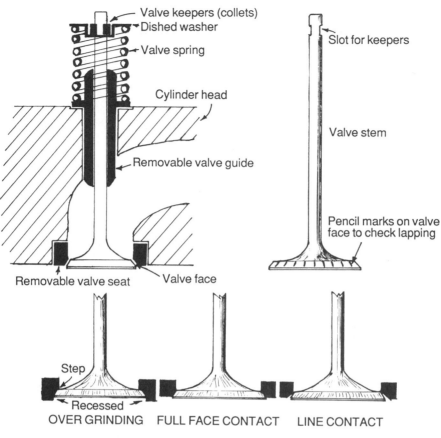

Figure 11-15. *Valves.*

Valves

Valves can be tested for leakage by laying the head on its side and pouring kerosene or diesel into the valve ports. If a valve is bad, the liquid will dribble out where the valve rests on its seat. If no leak is present, or only a tiny seepage, you may be wise to leave the valve in place and merely clean the carbon off its face and out of its port.

If leakage is present, the valve will have to be reground. Valves are usually held in place by two *keepers* (or collets), small semicircles of metal that lock in a slot cut into the valve stem (Figure 11-15). The keepers are held against the valve stem by a dished metal washer on top of the valve spring. In order to remove the keepers, the valve spring must be compressed so that the dished washer can be pushed down out of the way. Then the keepers are removed and the spring is released. The dished washer and spring will slide up and off the valve stem, and the valve can then be pushed out of the other side of the cylinder head.

A special tool—a valve-spring compressor or clamp—is used to remove valves from a cylinder head. This is essentially a large C-clamp that fits over the cylinder head, one end resting on the valve face and the other slotting over the valve stem and around the top of the spring. When the clamp is closed, it compresses the spring down the valve stem, allowing the keepers to be picked off. The clamp is then released, the spring slides off the valve stem, and the valve can be pushed out of the cylinder head.

Valve-spring clamps can be rented from automotive parts stores. Most are sufficiently adjustable to fit a wide range of cylin-

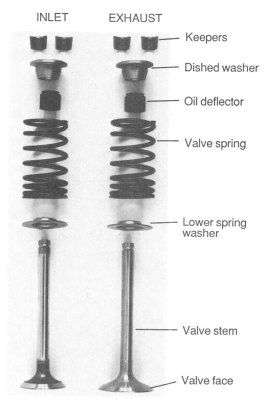

INLET   EXHAUST

— Keepers

— Dished washer

— Oil deflector

— Valve spring

— Lower spring washer

— Valve stem

— Valve face

Figure 11-16. *Inlet and exhaust valve components. (Courtesy Perkins Engines Ltd.)*

Figure 11-17. *Using a valve spring compressor. (This is a slightly different tool than that described in the text, but it serves the same purpose.) (Courtesy Perkins Engines Ltd.)*

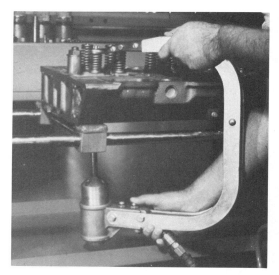

Figure 11-18. *An hydraulically operated valve spring compressor in a large machine shop. (Courtesy Caterpillar Tractor Co.)*

der heads, but if at all possible it is just as well to take the head to the store and check the available clamps for the best fit.

In an emergency, it is possible (though difficult) to push down on the valve spring with a suitably sized box-end wrench, allowing a second person to remove the keepers. This is easier with older, slower-revving engines, which tend to have weaker valve springs. The trick is to pick off the keepers without allowing the wrench to slip on the spring; any slippage usually results in the spring shooting off the stem and the tiny little keepers getting lost. Keepers are hard to buy and easy to lose—they need to be handled with care. It should be stressed that this is an emergency procedure undertaken at one's own risk; owners who intend to do their own decoking would be well advised to buy an appropriate valve-spring clamp.

The key area of a valve is the beveled region that sits on the valve seat in the cylin-der head (see Figure 11-15). If either the valve or seat are pitted in the area of contact, the head will have to go to a machine shop for regrinding of the seat and refacing of the valve. Exhaust valves need checking more

Figure 11-19. *Valve failure: corrosion from moisture and acids. (Courtesy Caterpillar Tractor Co.)*

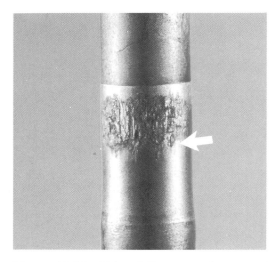

Figure 11-20. *Valve failure: metal to metal transfer (galling) from a valve stem sticking in its guide. (Courtesy Caterpillar Tractor Co.)*

Figure 11-21. *Valve failure: stress cracks caused by high temperature. (Courtesy Caterpillar Tractor Co.)*

closely than inlet valves because they are subject to much higher temperatures, and the exhaust gases tend to burn them more quickly. The exhaust valve closest to the exhaust manifold exit pipe is frequently the most corroded on a marine engine as a result of water vapor from a water-cooled exhaust coming back up the exhaust pipe.

If the seat and valve face are reasonably smooth, the valve can frequently be *lapped* back in by hand, as discussed in the next paragraph, although this is less feasible with the Stellite-faced valves and seats increasingly common in modern engines. These are especially hardened for long life, and while they can be lapped in by hand (with difficulty) to

Figure 11-22. *Valve failure: valve badly burned by escaping gases. (Courtesy Caterpillar Tractor Co.)*

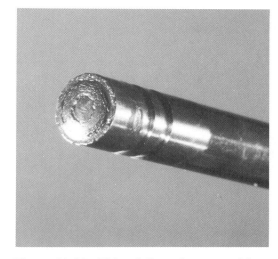

Figure 11-24. *Valve failure: beaten and battered valve stem end from an excessive valve clearance adjustment. (Courtesy Caterpillar Tractor Co.)*

Figure 11-23. *Valve failure: damage caused by a foreign object bouncing around in the combustion chamber. (Courtesy Caterpillar Tractor Co.)*

Figure 11-25. *Valve failure: a slightly bent valve. Notice the uneven grind marks on the face. (Courtesy Caterpillar Tractor Co.)*

alleviate minor problems, they cannot be machined in any way without abrading the Stellite. Thus, any problems that cannot be solved with minor grinding will require new valves and probably new seats.

To lap in a valve, apply a thin band of medium grinding paste (available from any automotive parts store) around the seating surface. Drop the valve back into the cylinder head, and place a lapping tool (essentially a rubber suction cup with a handle, available from any auto parts store) on the face of the valve. Spin the handle backward and forward between the palms of your hands while maintaining a gentle downward pressure to hold the valve against its seat. Every so often lift the valve off its seat,

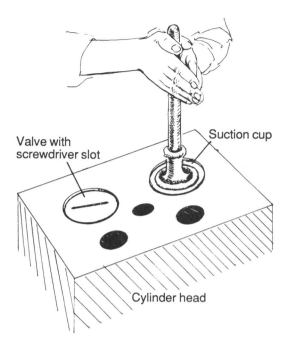

Figure 11-26. *Hand lapping a valve.*

Figure 11-27. *Checking for overgrinding of valves. (Courtesy Perkins Engines Ltd.)*

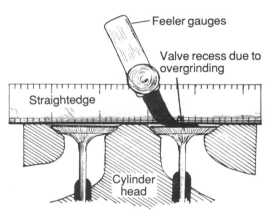

Figure 11-28. *Cutaway view of checking valves for overgrinding.*

rotate it a quarter of a turn or so, drop it back down, and work backward and forward some more. This ensures an even grinding of the valve and its seat, regardless of the position of the valve (see Figure 11-26). Some valves have a screwdriver slot in them, and the suction cup is unnecessary.

Continue this procedure until a line of clean metal is visible all the way around the valve and its seat. More grinding paste should be added as necessary. As soon as this line appears, the surfaces are polished in the same manner using a little fine grinding paste.

You can check the fit of a valve in its seat by making a series of pencil marks across the face of the valve about an eighth of an inch apart, then dropping the valve onto its seat. All the pencil marks should be cut by the seat (Figure 11-15).

Do not overgrind the valves. The objective is a thin line of continuous contact between the valve and seat—not a perfect fit. Overgrinding lowers the valve in the head, which increases the size of the combustion chamber and leads to a loss of compression. Once the valves and seats have been ground

beyond a certain point, the loss of compression becomes unacceptable and necessitates a major cylinder head overhaul. On many engines, the valve seats are separate inserts pressed into the cylinder head, and can be removed and replaced. Combined with new valves and valve guides (see below) this produces, for all intents and purposes, a new cylinder head. This work can only be done by a qualified machine shop.

The valve guide holds the valve in alignment in the cylinder head. A buildup of carbon around the valve stem and in the guide will sometimes cause valves to stick in their guides. These areas must be carefully cleaned during a decoke. Excessive wear in a guide will allow lubricating oil from the rocker arm to run down the valve stem and into the valve port, where it will be sucked into the engine and burned (in the case of an inlet valve), or burned by the hot exhaust gases (in the case of an exhaust valve). Valve guide and stem wear can be checked by attempting to rock the valve from side to side in its guide—no lateral movement is permissible. Most engines have replaceable valve guides, which are pressed into the cylinder head, but this is a job for the machine shop.

Replacement of valves is a reversal of removal. *It is essential to first wash away all traces of grinding paste by thoroughly flushing the cylinder head and components with diesel fuel or kerosene.* When refitted, the valves can once again be given the kerosene test to check their seating.

At this point, you should probably test older engines for overgrinding. To do this, lay a straightedge across the face of the cylinder head over the top of the valve and measure with a feeler gauge the extent to which the valve is recessed into the head (Figures 11-27 and 11-28). Check the degree of valve indentation against the manufacturer's specified limits to determine if the head needs new valves and seats.

Before you replace any valves, the springs should be visually checked for any cracks or corrosion. The length of each spring should be checked against the manufacturer's specification, if possible, or compared to a new spring. Replace the spring if it is short.

Pistons and cylinders

Pistons are sealed in their cylinders by piston rings. Areas in which significant wear occurs are the cylinder wall, the outer surface of the piston ring, and the width of the groove in the piston in which the ring sits. This groove will widen over time as a result of the rings working up and down as the piston moves in the cylinder.

When a piston is at the top of its stroke, its topmost ring is still a little way down the cylinder. Because the cylinder wears only where it is in contact with the rings, this top part of the cylinder will be unworn. A significantly worn cylinder bore will have a step at the top. In order to check this, rotate the crankshaft until the piston is at or near the bottom of its stroke. Clean away the carbon that has collected at the top of the bore, and run your fingernail up and down the first half-inch of the bore. If this step approaches the thickness of a fingernail, you should have the bores professionally measured to

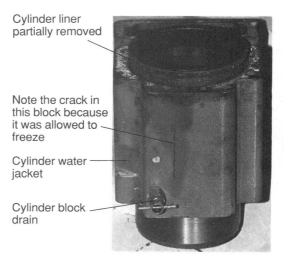

Cylinder liner partially removed

Note the crack in this block because it was allowed to freeze

Cylinder water jacket

Cylinder block drain

Figure 11-29. *Volvo MD17C cylinder with wet liner partially removed.*

Cylinder water jacket

Cylinder liner

Cylinder block drain

Figure 11-30. *Volvo MD17C cylinder with wet liner completely removed.*

determine whether the time has come for a cylinder renewal, which also includes new pistons and rings.

Other indications that a new cylinder is needed are any cracks, however small, or evidence of holes in the cylinder wall (such as erosion on the top flange of a wet cylinder liner). If the engine has experienced a piston seizure, the softer aluminum of the piston will frequently *peel* off and stick to the cylinder wall. This too will necessitate a new cylinder.

This is a good place to make the distinction between *wet* and *dry* cylinder liners. A wet liner is a sleeve pushed into the engine block and sealed at its top and bottom by O rings and gaskets. Wet cylinders are replaceable in the field without disturbing the engine block. Dry cylinders are a different kind of sleeve, pressed into a solid metal bore in the engine block. To replace them, the whole block has to be taken to a machine shop. All good diesel engines have wet cylinder liners, since these are far easier to replace in a major overhaul. This is of little concern to most pleasureboat owners, however, since it is rare for an engine to accumulate enough running time to require cylinder overhauls.

Piston removal

To remove a piston from its cylinder, its connecting rod must be detached from the crankshaft, and the piston and connecting rod pushed out through the top of the cylinder. Connecting rods are held to crankshafts by a cap, fastened with two bolts (Figure 11-31). On the majority of engines, gaining access to these two bolts requires removing the engine's oil pan, or sump, which is bolted to the underside of the crankcase. In most boats, you will have to remove the engine in order to get at the oil pan. A few marine diesels, however, provide access to the connecting rod caps through hatches in the side of the crankcase, allowing you to remove the pistons without disturbing the entire engine.

Lifting an engine from its bed is a major undertaking that involves breaking loose

much equipment (fuel lines, electrical connections, perhaps the exhaust system, the propeller coupling, etc.) and calls for some form of overhead crane or hoist. (On sailboats, the main boom, adequately supported, can often be used with an appropriate block and tackle.)

Sometimes it proves difficult to separate connecting rod caps from their connecting rods, even after the bolts are removed. *The two should never be pried apart.* Tap the cap gently with a soft hammer or block of wood while pulling down on it—this will invariably break it loose.

Before you take a piston from its cylinder any ridge of carbon at the top of the cylinder needs to be cleaned off. It is also a good idea to get hold of the connecting rod where it clamps around the crankshaft journal and to work the piston up and down and backward and forward. You will notice some sideways movement *along* the crankshaft journal, but

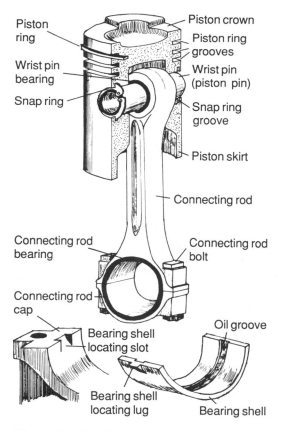

Figure 11-31. *Piston and connecting rod.*

otherwise this bearing should have no appreciable play. If there is, the engine will almost certainly have been knocking, and the bearing will need replacing.

When pistons are taken out and put back in you must take great care not to scratch the cylinder liner. Pistons *must* go back into the cylinder from which they came. The piston must face in the same direction; the connecting rod cap must go on the same way and the connecting rod bolts into the same holes. (On some engines new bolts must be fitted every time the caps are removed. This is a good practice for any engine.) The piston crown (top) should already be marked with its cylinder number and forward face, and the connecting rod and cap should also be numbered and marked. If not, some kind of identification needs to be made.

Pistons are cleaned commercially by using various solvents or blasting with glass beads. Assuming these are not available, a good soaking in diesel will help to loosen carbon and other deposits which can then be removed with very fine wet and dry sandpaper (400 grit) constantly wetted out with diesel. Care must be taken not to scratch pistons, which nowadays are mostly made of aluminum.

Once clean, pistons should be checked for excessive wear or damage. The following problems, with their likely causes, indicate that new pistons are called for:

1. A severely battered piston crown. This is generally caused by a broken or sticking valve, or a broken glow plug or injector tip.

2. Excessive cracking of the piston crown. The crown takes the full force of combustion and some hairline cracking is usual on modern high-speed diesels. On engines with pre-combustion chambers, this generally is concentrated at the point on the

Figure 11-33. *Cracking of the piston crown through overheating, in this case concentrated where the gases blow down out of the precombustion chamber. (Courtesy Caterpillar Tractor Co.)*

Figure 11-34. *Severe piston crown erosion due to a plugged air filter which led to erratic combustion. This piston is not re-usable. (Note the stainless steel plug in the center of the piston. It is placed at the point where the blow down gases from the precombustion chamber hit the crown, and helps to dissipate the heat. These plugs are found only on high performance engines.) (Courtesy Caterpillar Tractor Co.)*

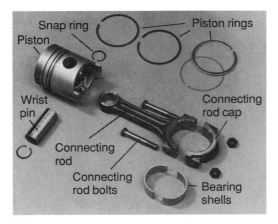

Figure 11-32. *A piston assembly. (Courtesy Perkins Engines Ltd.)*

Figure 11-35. *Generalized overheating of the crown. The top of the piston side has started to peel away and stick to the cylinder wall. Unlike the piston in Figure 11-36, this piston is not re-usable. (Courtesy Caterpillar Tractor Co.)*

Figure 11-37. *The skirt (base) of this piston has been skuffing (rubbing without lubrication) on the cylinder as a result of overheating. The skirt is beginning to break up and the piston is not re-usable. (Courtesy Caterpillar Tractor Co.)*

Figure 11-36. *Carbon cutting around the piston top from the ring of carbon at the top of the cylinder. The piston, though scratched, is not breaking up and can be re-used after cleaning. (Courtesy Caterpillar Tractor Co.)*

Figure 11-38. *This piston has been seizing from top to bottom through serious overheating or lubrication failure. It is not re-usable. (Courtesy Caterpillar Tractor Co.)*

piston crown where the combustion gases drive out of the pre-combustion chamber and hit the piston. However, extensive crazing or deep cracks mean that the piston top has overheated and the piston must be replaced. The most likely cause is faulty fuel injection.

3. Parts of a piston crown may be eaten away, also as a result of faulty injection. Injector dribble causes late combustion and detonation, which in turn leads to burned exhaust valves and erosion of pistons, espe-

cially in the area of the crown closest to the exhaust valve (this is the result of continuing combustion during the exhaust cycle). A plugged air filter or defective turbocharger will also cause improper combustion, and can lead to more widespread burning of the piston crown.

4. A piston may become severely worn all around its sides from the crown down to the top ring. This indicates that the above problems have resulted in generalized overheating of the piston crown, causing it to ex-

Figure 11-39. *The rings on this piston are stuck in their grooves, leading to overheating, blow-by, and serious erosion of the side of the piston. It is not re-usable. (Courtesy Caterpillar Tractor Co.)*

Figure 11-40. *A skuffed liner from piston seizure. This liner is not re-usable. (Courtesy Caterpillar Tractor Co.)*

pand and rub against its cylinder wall. Some scratching of this portion of a piston is normal from rubbing against the carbon ridge at the top of the cylinder, but excessive wear will require a new piston. If the piston rings are also damaged or stuck in their grooves, blow-by of hot gases is likely to spread this wear (known as *skuffing*) down the sides of the piston.

5. The same skuffing on the base (*skirt*) of a piston is indicative of widespread overheating, most likely due to a failure of the cooling system or a lack of lubrication. Left unattended this will probably lead to a piston seizure, with the surface of the piston breaking up and sticking to the cylinder wall.

Piston rings

Assuming the piston is undamaged, the key things to be checked are piston ring wear and the fit of the rings in their grooves. The rings may well be stuck in the grooves with carbon and other gummy deposits, so the first task is to clean them.

Piston rings are extremely brittle and easily broken. You should loosen them in their grooves by carefully cleaning off excess carbon, and use plenty of penetrating fluids. After you have freed the rings, the ends have to be expanded (pried apart) to enlarge the diameter sufficiently to lift them off the piston. Proprietary tools are available for this, but if you cannot get one, a few strips of thin metal slipped under the ring as it expands out of its groove will make the job easy enough (Figure 11-41). Old hacksaw blades carefully ground down to remove any sharp edges work well. You must slide the ring off evenly—if it gets cocked, it will probably break.

While this is a simple procedure, great care must be taken in easing the rings out of their grooves. Expand them only the minimum amount necessary to slide them off the piston. *Incorrect removal and installation procedures are a major cause of piston ring failure.* In general, rings should be removed only if strictly necessary and should then be replaced with new ones to be on the safe side.

The two ends of the piston rings often have sharp points, so care must be taken to keep these from scratching the piston when taking the rings off, and putting them on. Once off, the rings and ring grooves in the piston will need cleaning. The latter present a special problem—they must not be scratched or widened since this will allow gases to blow past the rings when they are re-installed. Although it is frequently done, it is not a good idea to use a piece of an old piston ring for cleaning out the ring grooves; it is far better to make a scraper to fit the grooves out of a piece of hardwood.

Piston rings are made of cast iron, generally with a facing of chrome where they contact the cylinder wall. Anytime this

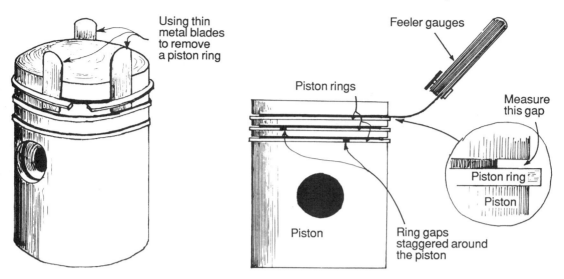

Figure 11-41. *Piston ring removal and checking.*

chrome is worn through the ring should be replaced, but since the action of a ring rubbing on its cylinder wall polishes its face, it is often hard to tell whether or not the chrome is gone. An indication of ring wear, though, can often be gained by looking at its side profile: rings are all either flat-faced, tapered, rounded (*barrel-faced*), or double-faced (oil scraper rings, always the bottom ring on a piston). Tapered and barrel-faced rings only contact a cylinder at the top of the taper or barrel. As wear increases the point of contact grows wider. If these rings are worn flat, with the whole ring width in contact with the cylinder wall, it is time to replace them. Double-faced rings can be compared with new ones to gauge the extent of wear.

To check piston ring wear, insert the ring into a cylinder and push it down to the bottom (no wear takes place at the bottom of the cylinder). Use an upside down piston as a plunger; it will keep the ring square, which is necessary for accurate measurement of wear. Feeler gauges are now used to measure the gap between the two ends of the ring. As a ring wears and pushes out on a cylinder wall, this gap increases. The size of the gap should be compared to the manufacturer's specifications to see if the wear is excessive. As a general rule it should be somewhere between

.003″ and .006″ per inch of cylinder diameter.

Piston rings are fitted to pistons using a reversal of the removal procedure. Most rings have a top and a bottom—the upper face should be marked as such. In any event, when they are taken off the top side should be noted, and they should go back the same way up.

Measure the wear of the piston ring groove by sliding the appropriate feeler gauge into the groove between the piston and the ring (Figure 11-44). As a general rule,

Figure 11-42. *Cleaning piston ring grooves with a piece of hardwood. (Courtesy Caterpillar Tractor Co.)*

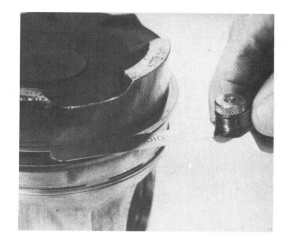

Figure 11-44. *Measuring piston ring to groove clearance. (Courtesy Caterpillar Tractor Co.)*

Figure 11-43. *Checking a piston ring gap. (Courtesy Perkins Engines Ltd.)*

this clearance should be about .003″ to .004″. Compare your measurements with the maker's specifications. Excessive clearance means that you may need a new piston.

Pistons are generally supplied in sets, sometimes complete with connecting rods, to keep the engine in balance and cut down on vibration. Each piston and rod assembly is machined to the same weight as all the others in the set, and if one piston needs replacing, it may prove necessary to change them all.

Because of the extremely close tolerances between the piston crown (top) and the cylinder head, new pistons for some engines are made oversize, and later machined in a lathe for an individual, exact fit in the cylinder. This is known as *topping*, and must be done by a specialist.

Piston ring bearings

Before you replace a piston, check for wear in the piston-pin bearing. The piston will be free to move from side to side on the pin, but if you detect any up-and-down movement in

the bearing, you will have to replace the piston-pin bushing in the connecting rod.

The piston pin is normally held in place by a snap ring at each end. These are spring-tensioned rings that expand into a groove machined into the piston. In order to remove these rings, you employ snap-ring pliers, which have hardened steel pins set in the end of each jaw. At each end of the snap ring is a small hole. Insert the tips of the pliers into the snap-ring holes and squeeze. If you don't have snap-ring pliers, you may be able to accomplish the job by grinding the jaws of needlenose pliers to the proper size to fit the snap-ring holes. Care must be taken to pinch up snap rings only enough to remove them. *Excessive squeezing and compression of snap rings is a major cause of later failure.*

You only need to remove the snap ring from one end of the piston pin. Then, if the piston pin does not slide out easily, *dip the piston into near-boiling water to expand it and it will be easy to tap out the pin.* Any attempt to force the pin out of a cold piston is likely to distort the piston permanently.

In order to push the old piston-pin bushing out of the connecting rod, you may have to heat the rod in near-boiling water as well. Then firmly support the connecting rod on blocks of wood, place the new bushing against the old one, hold a block of wood to

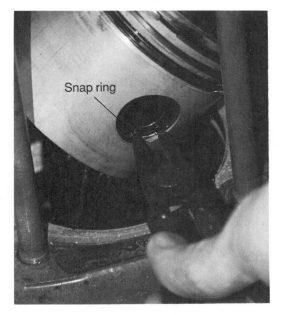

Figure 11-45. *Snap-ring pliers in action.*

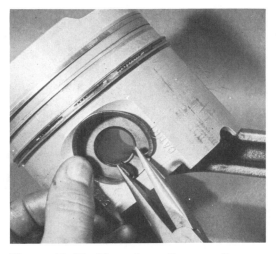

Figure 11-46. *Use of needlenose pliers to remove a snap ring. (Note that this snap ring has hooked ends, in contrast to the one with holes shown in Figure 11-45.) (Courtesy Caterpillar Tractor Co.)*

the new bushing, and gently tap the block with a hammer. The new bushing will drive out the old. The procedure will go more easily if you cool the new bushing in a freezer for a few minutes before starting.

Reassembly of the piston to its connecting rod is a reversal of disassembly, and may require the piston (but not the piston pin) to be heated once again. The pin can be put in a freezer or packed in ice, and will slide right into place. (The use of heat and ice at key points of engine assembly and disassembly can save a lot of frustration. The resulting one or two thousandths of an inch of expansion or contraction often turns an impossible task into a breeze.)

Connecting rod bearings

Now is also the time to replace the connecting rod bearings, if necessary. These bearings consist of a precision-made steel shell, lined with a special metal alloy (babbitt or lead bronze). The shells can be removed from the connecting rod and its cap by pushing on one end of each shell—they should slide around inside the rod or cap and slip

out the other end. A locating lug on the back of each shell at one end ensures that they can only be pushed out, and new ones inserted, in one direction.

If this is the engine's first major overhaul it will almost certainly have standard-sized bearings. But older engines may have had their crankshafts reground, in which case the crankshaft journal will be smaller than

Figure 11-47. *A set of bearing shells in good condition—light scratching is quite normal, as long as the bearing journal on the crankshaft is shiny and smooth. (Courtesy Caterpillar Tractor Co.)*

Figure 11-48. *Extensive scratching from dirt in the oil. These shells are not re-usable. (Courtesy Caterpillar Tractor Co.)*

Figure 11-49. *These shells are breaking up as a result of oil starvation. (Courtesy Caterpillar Tractor Co.)*

Figure 11-50. *Another case of oil starvation. This crankshaft will have to be removed from the engine and reground. (Courtesy Caterpillar Tractor Co.)*

Figure 11-51. *This shell got so hot that it began to melt. (Courtesy Caterpillar Tractor Co.)*

Figure 11-52. *This shell had a paint chip behind it due to improper cleaning at the time of installation. This resulted in severe localized overheating. It is not re-usable. (Courtesy Caterpillar Tractor Co.)*

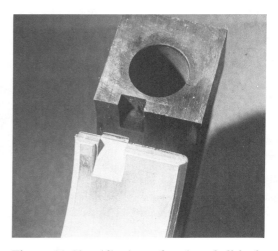

Figure 11-53. *Aligning a bearing shell locking tab with its housing. (Courtesy Caterpillar Tractor Co.)*

Figure 11-54. *Aligning a bearing shell oil hole with its oilway. (Courtesy Caterpillar Tractor Co.)*

Figure 11-55. *The markings on a piston crown. (Courtesy Perkins Engines Ltd.)*

standard and the bearing shells correspondingly thicker. The back of the shells will be stamped STD; .010; .020; or .030, indicating the size of the new shells required.

If the engine has been knocking very badly or the old bearing shells are seriously worn or scored, the crankshaft journal may be damaged or worn into an ellipse. The latter can only be measured with the appropriate micrometers, which will require a specialist's help. If the crankshaft is damaged or excessively worn, it is pointless to fit new bearing shells because they will only last a short while. The crankshaft will have to be removed and reconditioned, which is well beyond the scope of this book.

When fitting new bearing shells to a connecting rod and its cap, the backs of the shells and the seating surfaces on the rod and cap must be *spotlessly* clean. The new shells can be pushed directly onto their seats, or slid around inside their housings until the lugs seat in the slots. The shells must seat squarely and the lugs be correctly positioned. Make sure that any bearing shell that has an oil hole in it is fitted to the appropriate housing and lined up with its oilway.

Figure 11-56. *Lowering a piston into its cylinder. (Courtesy Perkins Engines Ltd.)*

Replacing pistons

When you put a piston back into the cylinder from which it came, the crank for that cylinder should be at bottom dead center. Coat the cylinder, piston, and rings with oil, then gently lower the piston into the bore until the bottom ring, the oil-scraper ring, rests on the top of the cylinder. At this point, all the rings should be arranged so that their end-gaps are staggered around the piston (Figure

Figure 11-57. *Use of a piston ring clamp. The clamp squeezes the piston rings into their grooves. (Courtesy Perkins Engines Ltd.)*

11-41). This prevents blow-by through lined-up end gaps.

Ring grooves on the pistons of 2-cycle engines have a pin in them at one point. This is placed in the middle of the ring gap and prevents the rings from turning on the piston, which might allow the ends of the rings to line up with the air-intake ports at the bottom of the cylinder. If this happened, the rings would try to spring out into the ports and would break.

A piston-ring clamp can be rented from an automobile parts store (provided you know the piston diameter) to hold the rings tightly in their grooves while the piston slides into its cylinder. It is relatively easy to dispense with the clamp, however, if you have available a helper and three screwdrivers or similar blunt instruments. The ring on which the piston is resting is pushed into its groove with one screwdriver at its center point (the point opposite the ring gap). The helper then works around the ring in one direction, easing it into its groove until almost at one end. He then also holds it in at that point with another screwdriver. The mechanic works around the ring in the other direction, doing

the same thing, and holds the other end in with the third screwdriver. Now the ring should be all the way in its groove, and the mechanic still has one hand free to tap the piston gently down into the cylinder, using the handle of a hammer or similar piece of wood (Figure 11-58).

The piston will slide down until the next ring sits on top of the cylinder, and the process is repeated. *Never use force*—it will merely result in broken rings. Once all the rings are in the cylinder, the piston is pushed down from above, and guided onto the crankshaft from below, making sure the connecting rod is lined up squarely with the crankshaft journal. The crankshaft journal (bearing surface) must be spotlessly clean (use *lint-free* rags) and well-oiled. Replace the connecting rod cap.

It is good practice to fit new cap bolts whether they are called for or not. These bolts are subjected to very high loads, and if one fails a tremendous amount of damage will result.

When the cap nuts and bolts are replaced they must be tightened to a very specific torque. This will be given in the manufacturer's specifications. A special wrench—a torque wrench—will have to be bought or borrowed to do this. These wrenches indicate exactly how much pressure is being applied to the nut or bolt.

Torque wrenches come in two basic types. On the more expensive ones, the end of the handle screws in and out, lining up a pointer with a scale *on the body* of the wrench. The scale indicates the torque pressure at which the wrench is now set. When the wrench is used it makes an audible click when this torque setting is reached.

Cheaper wrenches have a flexible handle with a pointer attached to it, the end of which moves over a scale set *across* the wrench. As pressure is applied to a nut or bolt the handle of the wrench flexes and the pointer moves across the scale. It is hard to use these wrenches with any degree of precision.

When you torque nuts or bolts the threads must be clean, free-running, and generally oiled (sometimes a manual will

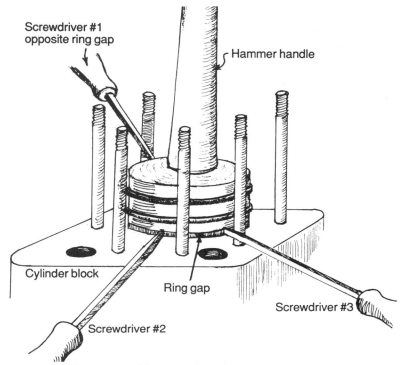

Screwdriver #1
opposite ring gap

Hammer handle

Cylinder block

Ring gap

Screwdriver #3

Screwdriver #2

Figure 11-58. *Piston replacement without a ring clamp.*

specify a *dry* torque setting, without oil). Friction in the threads will give a false reading on the torque wrench. The nuts or bolts must be pulled down with an even, steady pressure—sudden jerks on the wrench will also give false torque readings. On critical nuts and bolts it is not such a bad idea to over-torque them by just a few pounds, then back them off and re-torque to the specified point. This will ensure that everything is correctly pulled down.

At all critical bolt-tightening points in engine work, bolts must be tightened evenly. Just pinch one, and then do the bolt opposite; then apply a few more pounds of pressure to each one and continue in this fashion until the final torque setting is reached. This should be done in a *minimum* of three stages.

When you replace bearing caps anywhere in the engine, the shaft they enclose should be turned a full revolution by hand after each increase in the tightening pressure until full torque is reached. This is to ensure that there are no tight spots or binding. Tight

spots must be sorted out; this procedure is especially important when fitting new bearing shells.

Replacing cylinder heads

By now it should go without saying that the cylinder head and block must be spotlessly clean before you replace the head. Any pieces of rag and so on used to block off the oil, water, and other passages in the block and head must be removed at this time. Set a new gasket on the block and lower the head onto it. Some gaskets have a *top* and will be appropriately labeled. Although most manufacturers do not recommend it, metal gaskets often benefit from a little jointing paste smeared on them, taking care not to get any down the passages. (Jointing paste can be bought from any automotive parts store; be sure it is made for high temperature, is resistant to water and oil, and will withstand high pressure.) Most fiber gaskets (increasingly the norm) are fitted without any paste.

Figure 11-59. *A well-cleaned cylinder head face. (Courtesy Perkins Engines Ltd.)*

Always fit a new gasket if possible, even if the old one looks perfectly all right. It is tremendously aggravating to reassemble an engine with an old gasket only to find that it leaks.

The head nuts (bolts) must be tightened evenly, a bit at a time as outlined above, until the manufacturer's specified torque is reached (see your owner's manual). Proper torquing procedures are much more important here than on gasoline engines, owing to the much higher cylinder pressures generated by diesel engines. If the correct bolt tightening sequence is not followed, uneven pressure may develop and lead to a blown head gasket or a warped cylinder head. If the manufacturer's recommended torque sequence is not available, it is reasonably safe to assume that the center nuts are pulled down first. From then on, work out to the ends of the cylinder head, tightening a nut on one side of the center and then one on the other side, and so on until all are done. It is always a good idea to come back and

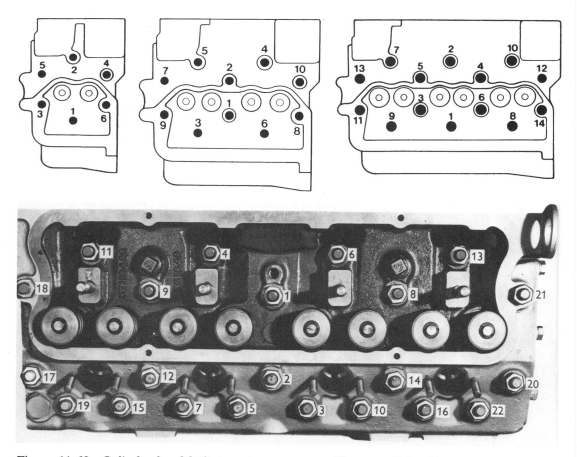

Figure 11-60. *Cylinder head bolt torquing sequence. (Courtesy Volvo Penta and Perkins Engines Ltd.)*

recheck the torque setting on these nuts after the engine has been reassembled and run for a while. A head gasket (especially metal ones) will occasionally settle, loosening the head nuts and creating the potential for a blown gasket.

Replacing push rods and rockers

Before you replace the push rods, roll them on a flat surface to make sure they are straight. A chart table or galley countertop provides an acceptable surface for such a test, as does the bed of a table saw or drill press. Any bend will be immediately apparent. Place the push rods into their respective holes in the cylinder head and block (rounded ends down, cupped ends up) and be sure each is properly seated in a hollow in what is known as a *cam follower*. This seat cannot be seen, but if you've missed it the push rod will be cockeyed, and will probably be resting on the rim of the cam follower. In some engines where the push rods share a common space, it is possible to miss the cam follower

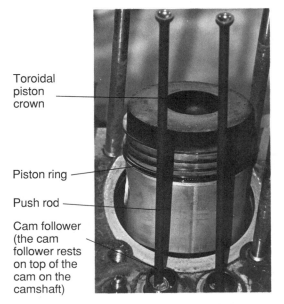

Toroidal piston crown

Piston ring

Push rod

Cam follower (the cam follower rests on top of the cam on the camshaft)

Figure 11-61. Push rods and cam followers. (The cylinder has been removed and the push rods have been wedged in place with paper to illustrate their location.)

altogether or even to hit the wrong one, but in most engines this cannot be done. If the push rod is centered in its hole in the cylinder head and feels firmly cupped at its lower end, it is seated correctly. Note that some push rods will be sticking up more than others.

The rockers go on next, but before fitting them the lock nut at the end of each rocker arm should be loosened and the screw it locks undone a couple of turns (Figure 11-66). This is just a little safety precaution in case the valve timing has been upset or valve clearances radically changed. It prevents any risk of forcing a valve down onto a piston crown and bending the valve stem when the rocker bolts are tightened up. Torque down the rocker gear to the manufacturer's setting.

Re-timing an engine

A decoke will not disturb the timing of an engine with push rods, but anytime an overhead camshaft is removed valve timing is upset. The fuel injection pump is tied in with the valve timing on all engines; therefore, the following procedure for re-timing an overhead camshaft coincidentally describes how to re-time a fuel injection pump on *any* engine.

Engine timing involves three gears: the timing drive gear, which is keyed to the end of the crankshaft; the camshaft drive gear, which operates the valve timing; and the fuel injection pump drive gear. On 2-cycle engines these gears are all the same size because the camshaft and fuel injection pump rotate at the same speed as the engine, but on 4-cycle engines the timing drive gear is half the size of the other two because the crankshaft has to rotate twice for every complete engine cycle.

The drive from the timing drive gear is transmitted to the other two by belt, chain, or intermediate gears. Engine timing consists of getting these three gears in *exactly* the correct relationship to one another. Each of the gears involved in engine timing has a punch mark or line somewhere on its face. When engine timing is belt-driven or chain-driven, these marks are lined up with corresponding marks on the timing-gear housing and then the belt or chain is slipped on and tensioned. Always double-check to see that all the marks are still lined up after belt or chain tensioning—sometimes one of the gears will move around by one tooth, in which case timing will have to be repeated.

When engine timing is transmitted through intermediate gears, these intermediate gears will have punch marks that line up with the marks on the timing gears (Figure 11-64). This alignment should be *exact*—if it is not, something is wrong.

Timing is always done at top dead center (TDC) on the compression stroke of the #1 cylinder, the one at the front end, or timing gear end, of the engine. When the engine is at TDC on the #1 cylinder, the keyway in the end of the crankshaft, which positions the timing drive gear, will also be at TDC.

On 2-cycle engines there is only one TDC because the engine fires on every revolution of the crankshaft, but 4-cycle engines have two TDCs—one on the compression stroke and one on the exhaust stroke. Engine timing is done at TDC on the compression stroke. Normally you can determine which stroke is which by looking at the position of the valves, but with the camshaft off this is not possible.

If the fuel injection pump timing has not been disturbed, the mark on its drive gear

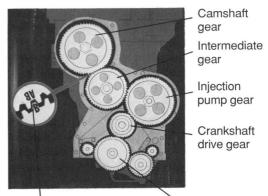

Timing marks on the gears — Oil pump and other miscellaneous gears

Camshaft gear

Intermediate gear

Injection pump gear

Crankshaft drive gear

Figure 11-62. *Engine timing marks. (Courtesy Caterpillar Tractor Co.)*

Camshaft

Fuel injection pump

Drive gear

Oil pump and other miscellaneous gears

Figure 11-63. *Engine timing gears.*

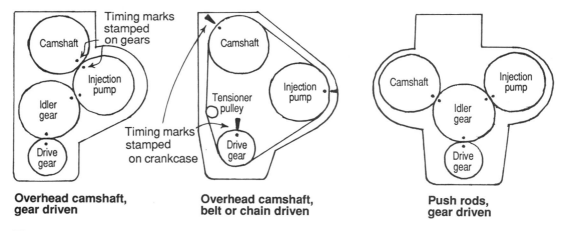

Timing marks stamped on gears

Camshaft

Injection pump

Idler gear

Drive gear

Timing marks stamped on crankcase

Overhead camshaft, gear driven

Camshaft

Tensioner pulley

Injection pump

Drive gear

Overhead camshaft, belt or chain driven

Camshaft

Injection pump

Idler gear

Drive gear

Push rods, gear driven

Figure 11-64. *Engine timing arrangements.*

will line up with a corresponding mark on the timing gear housing or an intermediate gear when the engine is at TDC on the compression stroke of the #1 cylinder. From this, you will be able to establish the correct TDC. If the fuel pump timing has been disturbed then it does not matter at which TDC the #1 cylinder is because the camshaft and fuel pump will be timed together. *It is essential that the timing of the fuel injection pump and valves be done at the same TDC*—which one is immaterial. Otherwise it would be possible to have the injection pump injecting the cylinders when the pistons were at the top of their exhaust strokes; the engine would never run. This is known as the timing being 180° out—although the engine is a full revolution (360°) out, the camshaft and injection pump only turn at half engine speed on 4-cycle engines and so one of them would be 180° out.

With the engine at TDC on the #1 cylinder and the crankshaft keyway also at TDC,

Figure 11-65. *Fuel injection pump (CAV type DPA), mounted vertically. (Courtesy Perkins Engines Ltd.) 1. The timing marks scribed on the pump mounting flange and the engine timing cover. 2. The idle speed adjusting screw. 3. The maximum speed screw. (This must not be tampered with. Although it cannot be seen in this photograph, there is a seal on it which, if broken, automatically voids the engine warranty.)*

line up all the gear marks with their corresponding marks on the gear housing or intermediate gears, then install the belt, chain, or intermediate gears. Basic timing is complete. All that remains to do is to fine-tune the fuel injection pump timing.

The fuel injection pump timing gear is either keyed to the pump drive shaft or fits onto a splined shaft with a master spline. In either event, it can go on only one way (the same is true for the valve timing gear). The timing is then set up as described above.

In almost all instances, the injection pump will be bolted to the other side of the timing gear housing. (On occasion it is bolted to a little platform of its own.) The flange on the pump that bolts up to the gear housing has machined slots for its bolts, which means that even after the gear timing has been set up, the pump can still be rotated to the extent allowed by the slots. This rotation does not move the timing gear but turns the pump around its drive shaft.

A line scribed on the pump flange and the timing gear housing *must be exactly lined up before the pump flange is tightened*. This completes injection pump timing.

Valve clearances, 4-cycle engines

All valves have a small clearance, when fully closed, between the valve stem and rocker arm. It is important to maintain the manufacturer's specified clearance. If the clearance is too little, as the engine heats up and all the metal parts expand a valve may stay slightly open at all times, resulting in lost compression and burned valves and seats. If, on the other hand, the clearance is too great, valve openings will be slightly delayed, the valve will not open far enough, and the valve will close a little too soon.

On a 4-cycle engine, the inlet valve opens on a downward stroke of the piston. Both valves are then closed during the next upward (compression) stroke, and for most of the following downward (power) stroke. The exhaust valve then opens and remains open on the next upward (exhaust) stroke. At the top of this stroke the exhaust valve is closing *at the same time* as the inlet valve is opening. This is known as *valve overlap* and the valves are said to be *rocking*. By watching the movement of the rocker arms while you slowly rotate the engine, you can determine where in the cycle each cylinder is, and therefore, the position of the cam that operates each push rod.

Set a valve clearance when the valve is fully closed at TDC on the compression stroke. On engines with overhead camshafts you can see the cams, and the valve clearances should be set when a cam is 180° away from the rocker arm it operates. On engines with push rods, where the operation of the camshaft cannot be observed, the following method will establish the correct point for setting valve clearances.

In order to find top dead center for any cylinder, slowly rotate the crankshaft and watch the inlet-valve push rod as it moves up and down. When it is almost all the way down, the piston is at the bottom of the inlet stroke. Mark the crankshaft pulley, and turn the engine another half a revolution. Now the piston will be close to TDC on its compression stroke, and you can set the valve clearances. (On most engines, the crankshaft pulley is marked for TDC on the #1 cylinder, but on older engines you should not rely on

any mark—someone may have changed things around at some time.)

The manufacturer's specifications will indicate valve clearances in millimeters or thousandths of an inch, and whether the valves should be adjusted hot or cold. If they are to be set when the engine is hot, an initial adjustment will have to be made cold, and then checked again after the engine has been run. Place an appropriate feeler gauge between the top of the valve stem and the rocker arm (Figure 11-66). The adjusting screw on the rocker arm (which was previously loosened) is tightened down until the arm just begins to pinch the feeler gauge. The lock nut on the adjusting screw is then tightened, and the clearance is double-checked in case something slipped. This valve is set, and the other one on the same cylinder is now done.

On a two-cylinder engine, when one piston is at TDC the other is at BDC. After the valves on one cylinder are set, a half-turn will bring the piston on the other cylinder to TDC. A quick glance at the push rods will show if this is TDC on the exhaust or the compression stroke—if it is the former, the engine will need to be rotated another full turn. The valve clearances on the second cylinder can now be set.

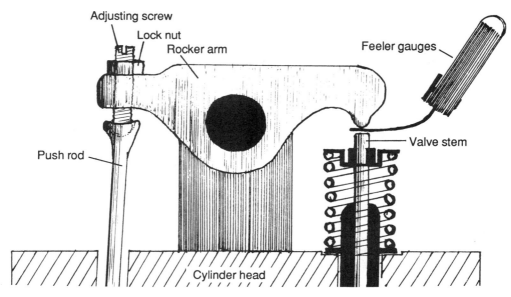

Figure 11-66. *Setting valve clearances.*

On three-cylinder and six-cylinder in-line engines, one-third of a revolution will always bring another piston to TDC. The pistons of six-cylinder in-line engines move in pairs— normally numbers one and six together, two and five, and three and four. When one pair is at TDC on its exhaust stroke (i.e. the valves are rocking), another pair will be at TDC on its compression stroke and you can set the valves.

On four-cylinder in-line engines the pistons also move in pairs—1 and 4 together, and 2 and 3—with a half-turn separating TDC between the pairs. When the valves on either one of a pair of pistons are rocking, the other piston in the pair is at TDC on its compression stroke and its valves can be set.

If you are at all unsure of how this works, it helps to write down all the cylinders on a piece of paper, showing which ones operate together. The inlet and exhaust valves should be determined (from their respective manifolds) and the engine turned over slowly a few times to familiarize yourself with the valve opening and closing sequence. Careful attention to the logic of the situation will soon indicate where the pistons are and when to set valve clearances. (Note:

If the engine is being turned over by hand, make absolutely certain that it is turned over the right way.)

Valve clearances, 2-cycle engines

Two-cycle engines have no inlet valves, only exhaust valves. Many have two exhaust valves per cylinder. Remember that these valves open toward the bottom of the power stroke and close partway up the compression stroke. From the point of closure, another one-third of a turn will bring the piston more or less to TDC, and the valve clearances can be set.

Accessory equipment

The final step in a decoke is to refit all the fuel lines, manifolds, valve cover, turbocharger, and anything else that was removed. If no other part of the fuel system has been broken loose, a few turns of the engine should push diesel up to the injectors. Otherwise the fuel system will need bleeding, as previously explained.

Chapter Twelve

Overhauls, Part Two

The cooling system

The cooling system normally requires very little attention, with the exception of the raw-water strainer. This should be checked at regular intervals as a matter of routine maintenance—perhaps whenever the oil is changed. Should the engine show signs of overheating, the obvious first suspect is a plugged raw-water strainer. All parts of the cooling system through which raw water passes need to be protected from electrolysis with suitable zinc anodes. These too will need checking, and changing, if necessary, at regular intervals.

In time, silt and sand may block the tubes in a heat exchanger or build up in the block of a raw-water-cooled engine. The engine will show a slow, but steady, rise in temperature. A heat exchanger is easily cleaned out by removing the two end caps and flushing the tubes. In extreme cases, you may need to push a rod through the tubes to clear blockages, but take care not to damage the relatively soft cupro-nickel tubing.

Raw-water-cooled engines can only be flushed out by removing some item from the block that will give access to the cooling passages, opening up the cylinder block drain (or better still, removing it to create a larger hole), and holding a hose pipe to the block with as much pressure as possible. On occasion, various salts crystalize out of the raw water onto cylinder walls and internal pas-sages, and these can only be removed with special solutions. This requires a specialist's advice. (I once worked on a 2,000-h.p. engine with a salt problem. A special solution was used to dissolve the salts, and was not properly flushed out. The engine cooling system was then filled with an antifreeze solution. The two chemicals reacted to precipitate out an insoluble chemical goo that completely plugged the entire engine. Two months and several chemical companies later no one had been able to find a chemical that would dissolve the goo without eating away some of the engine.)

Engines with raw-water cooling need draining in cold weather. Be sure to catch all the low spots in the system. The raw water side of a heat exchanger also needs draining. With a heat exchanger, the engine coolant can be mixed with antifreeze, just as in an automobile. It is wise to change the antifreeze every year. Although it gives indefinite protection against freeze up, certain anti-corrosion inhibitors contained in it get used up, and these need periodic replenishing.

When an engine is started after any part of the cooling system has been drained, double-check the flow of cooling water to the engine, especially with raw-water cooling. If a water pump is air-bound or coolant fails to circulate for any other reasons, it does not take very long to do extensive damage (a cracked cylinder head, for example).

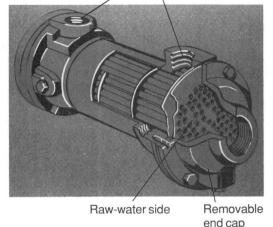

Engine cooling water
side, "in" and "out"

Raw-water side   Removable
end cap

Figure 12-1. *A typical heat exchanger.
(Courtesy Caterpillar Tractor Co.)*

Figure 12-3. *A cracked cylinder block (with
the liner removed). The engine was allowed
to freeze.*

An air-bound cooling system is bled just like a fuel system, starting from the water source and working up to the pump. Once the pump is primed, it should purge the rest of the system.

Water pumps are generally of the piston, diaphragm, or rubber impeller type on raw-water systems, and frequently of the centrifugal type (standard on automobiles) on closed (heat exchanger) cooling systems. The latter rarely give problems, and then are simply exchanged for a new unit.

Piston type pumps operate in a fashion similar to an engine piston, sucking water into a cylinder through an inlet valve, and pushing it back out through a discharge valve on the next stroke. The piston is generally sealed in its cylinder by a rubber O ring, or on some older engines, a leather dished washer bolted to the bottom of the piston. These are the only items likely to cause trouble. What often happens is that an engine is drained and closed up for the winter, and then sits for several months. The O ring, or leather, becomes stuck to the pump cylinder wall. When the engine is restarted in the spring, it tears. The puzzled owner knows everything was functioning just fine last October and can't make out

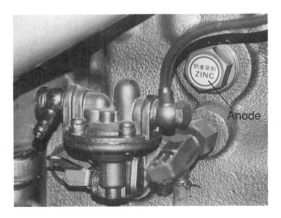

Figure 12-2. *A zinc anode in the cooling
system of a Yamaha diesel engine.*

Figure 12-4. *A raw-water pump from a
Volvo MD 17C.*

Drive gear   Pump impeller

Figure 12-5. *Cutaway of an engine-mounted centrifugal water pump. (Courtesy Caterpillar Tractor Co.)*

why no water is passing through the cooling system.

Diaphragm water pumps operate in just the same way as diaphragm fuel lift pumps. The only likely point of failure is the diaphragm. The pumps generally have a hole in the base and if the diaphragm fails, water will dribble out of this hole. Diaphragms are easily replaced by removing the pump cover. Piston- and diaphragm-type pumps have inlet and discharge valves. If the valves become worn or fail to seat, the pump will not operate properly and overheating will occur.

On occasion, all the impeller blades on a rubber impeller-type pump will strip off (normally after the winter once again, or if it has been run dry). You can replace the impeller by simply removing the pump cover, but all the broken blades must be tracked down to prevent them from blocking some vital cooling passage. At other times the impeller may be intact but the keyway or spline holding it to its shaft may be stripped off or broken so that it fails to turn when the shaft turns. Figure 12-6 shows an impeller-type pump.

Once in a while an engine with a heat exchanger will overheat, and a thorough analysis implicates the thermostat. The thermostat housing is almost always near the top of the engine, at the front (the crankshaft pulley end), with one or more cooling water hoses coming out of it. Generally it is held down with a couple of bolts; once these are removed, the housing is gently pried up. The thermostat can be lifted out and tested by placing it in a pot of cool water and warming it. A thermometer will indicate whether the thermostat begins to open in the correct range—generally around 165°F on engines with heat exchangers, and around 145°F on engines with raw-water cooling (if a thermostat is fitted at all). Thermostats are relatively cheap, and if you go to the trouble of taking yours out, you might just as well replace it.

The fuel injection system

The only user-serviceable parts of a fuel injection system are the fuel strainer and rubber diaphragm in the lift pump, and the diaphragm found in some fuel injection pumps.

Lift pump. The body has a drain hole in its base. If the diaphragm fails, fuel will normally dribble out of this hole. This prevents the fuel from entering the engine and diluting the engine oil. (Recent Coast Guard reg-

Figure 12-6. *An impeller-type water pump (JABSCO 5330-9001). (Courtesy ITT Jabsco)*

Temperature sensing pickup

Thermostat housing bolts

Figure 12-7. *Thermostat housing on a Volvo MD 17C.*

Thermostat

Figure 12-8. *Thermostat removed from a Volvo MD 17C.*

ulations call for the elimination of this bleed hole.) Diaphragm replacement and screen cleaning are simply done by removing the pump cover. The fuel system will then have to be bled.

Diaphragm fuel injection pumps. As mentioned in Chapter 5, a few engines have vacuum-type governors. In this case the injection pump has a diaphragm in the back of it. This diaphragm pushes against the fuel-control rack on one side, and is controlled by a vacuum line to the air inlet manifold on the other side. A holed diaphragm can lead to a loss of power, excessive black smoke, a very rough idle and over-speeding.

Testing a fuel pump diaphragm is a simple procedure. It should be done with the engine off. The diaphragm is contained in a round housing at the back of the pump, the end not attached to the engine. Coming out of the top of this housing is a vacuum sensing line that leads to the air-inlet manifold.

This line needs to be disconnected at the pump.

At the opposite end of the pump, just above the flange that holds it to the engine, will be a protective cap, inside of which is the fuel-control rack. Remove this cap. On the side of the pump, below and just forward of the vacuum line, is the pump-control lever (throttle). Hold this in the stop position.

If you place a finger tightly over the vacuum connection on the pump (where the vacuum line was disconnected) and let go the control-rod lever (throttle), the fuel-control rack at the engine end of the pump (where the protective cap was removed) should move a short distance then stop (as long as the vacuum fitting is kept blocked by your finger). If there are any leaks in the diaphragm or around the seal to its housing, the control rack will keep moving (perhaps slowly) until it is out as far as it can go. In this case the diaphragm needs inspecting, and probably replacing.

You can get to it by removing its cover

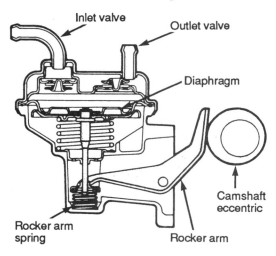

A mechanical fuel pump is mechanically actuated by a rocker arm or push rod without electrical assistance.

The rocker arm spring holds the rocker arm in constant contact with the camshaft or eccentric. As the end of the rocker arm moves upward, the other end of the arm pulls the fuel diaphragm downward. The vacuum action of the diaphragm enlarges the fuel chamber drawing fuel from the fuel tank through the inlet valve and into the fuel chamber.

The return stroke starting at the high point of the cam releases the compressed diaphragm spring, expelling fuel through the outlet valve.

When the immediate fuel needs of the engine are satisfied, pressure builds in the fuel line and pump chamber. This pressure forces the diaphragm/piston to make shorter and shorter strokes, until more fuel is needed in the engine.

Certain mechanical fuel pumps have hand priming capabilities. Hand priming is accomplished by repeatedly depressing the hand primer until fuel has filled the system.

Figure 12-9. *A typical mechanical fuel pump. (Courtesy AC Spark Plug Division, G.M. Corp.)*

(four screws) and undoing the bolt holding it to the fuel rack mechanism.

Injection pump oil reservoirs. While most pumps are lubricated with diesel fuel, some in-line jerk pumps have an oil sump with regular engine oil in it. This becomes diluted with diesel over time and occasionally needs changing. The sump will have an oil drain plug and either a dipstick or level plug. In the latter case, take out the level plug and fill the sump with oil until it runs out of the plug hole. Replace the plug. *No other area of the fuel pump is serviceable in the field, and it should be left strictly alone.*

Injectors. Lucas CAV recommends, "In the absence of specific data, a figure of 900 hours of operating between servicing is a useful guide for the boat owner." Aside from pulling the injectors to have them serviced, injectors should be left well alone. Individual injector needle valves are matched to their bodies to within 0.00004″ (four one-hundred thousandth of an inch). Equipment of this degree of precision needs to be disassembled by specialists. "It is not possible for the owner or crew to recondition or service an injector without the essential nozzle setting outfit, special tools, technical data and service training," states the CAV handbook. "Any tampering or attempts at servicing without these essentials will always make matters worse." The following information is therefore given only for those in a dire emergency and after all other procedures have failed to solve a problem.

Servicing of a fuel injection system requires *extreme cleanliness.* Before you attempt to break loose fuel lines or remove injectors, the area around them should be thoroughly cleaned off. *The instant any fuel lines are disconnected both loose connections must be capped.* Once an injector is removed from a cylinder head its hole must be temporarily plugged to prevent dirt from falling in the cylinder.

Injectors are either held in place by a metal plate bolted to the cylinder head, or they are screwed directly into the head. The former can sometimes be hard to break loose —dribble a little penetrating oil down the

Injector nut   Leak-off pipe

Glow plug   Thermostat housing

Figure 12-10. *Screw-in-type injectors.*

side of the injector an hour or two before it is pulled out.

On some engines (for example, the Volvo Penta series 2000) the injector is in a sleeve that is directly cooled by the engine cooling circuit. Occasionally the sleeve sticks to the injector and comes out with it. The block should therefore be drained of coolant before attempting to pull any injectors, so that there is no risk of coolant running into a cylinder. Should the sleeve come out, the cylinder head will have to go to a dealer, since installation of a new sleeve requires special tools.

Injectors, and many fuel lines, are sealed with copper washers. Be careful not to lose any of these, and be sure that they go back in the right place on reassembly.

Once an injector is out of the cylinder head, you can check its operation by reconnecting it to its injection line, bleeding the line, cranking the engine over, and observing the spray pattern (but only after the fuel

lines to the other injectors have been loosened to prevent the engine from starting). The engine should be rotated at a speed of at least 60 rpm. Each type of injector will produce a distinct spray pattern, but all should have certain features in common:

1. a high degree of atomization of the diesel;
2. a strong, straight-line projection of the spray from the nozzle as a fine mist and with no visible steaks of unvaporized fuel;
3. no dribbling or drops of fuel (the nozzle tip should remain dry after injection is complete);
4. the fuel should come out of all the holes in the nozzle in even proportions.

Figure 12-11 illustrates different spray patterns.

Whenever an injector is tested in this manner, you must keep well out of the way. The diesel fuel is fine enough, and has more than enough force, to penetrate the skin and blood vessels, and it can cause severe blisters and blood poisoning.

If the spray pattern is defective or the nozzle drips, the injector nozzle needs cleaning. It may prove sufficient to clean the carbon off the outside of the nozzle and to use a very fine wire to clear the holes in the nozzle. A brush of *brass* bristles and diesel fuel should be used on the nozzle—steel brushes should never be used because they can damage the holes in the nozzle. If a proper set of injector-hole cleaning prickers is not available, a strand of copper wire may work (or perhaps the pricker off a primus stove or kerosene lantern). Take care not to enlarge any holes and not to break off a pricker in an injector hole.

If an injector is to be disassembled, first soak it for several hours in Gunk or diesel fuel to loosen everything up. Bosch stipulates a *minimum* of four hours. Two ounces of caustic soda dissolved in one pint of water with half an ounce of detergent will go to work on carbon. This volume of caustic soda must not be exceeded or corrosion is possible. The parts to be decarbonized are boiled

Finely atomized spray pattern.

One hole plugged leading to a streaky injection spray with drops of unvaporized fuel.

Post injection "dribble."

Figure 12-11. *Abnormal spray patterns.*

in this solution for an hour, continually topping up the water to compensate for any that evaporates. Before you reassemble the injector, it will need thorough flushing and drying to remove all traces of the caustic soda.

In order to disassemble an injector, you will have to hold the injector body firmly. A special vise is recommended, although it will probably not be available. *The injector must not be directly clamped up in a steel vise since this may distort it.* Remember how *precise* everything is. Protective wooden blocks should be placed around the injector body, and the vise given only the minimum necessary pressure.

Within an injector is a powerful spring (see Figure 12-12). Sometimes the spring pressure is externally adjustable (as illustrated) by removing a cap nut on the top of the injector. If this is the case, the spring adjusting locknut and screw should be backed off *an exact number of turns carefully counted* until the spring is no longer under tension. This spring determines the pressure at which the injector opens and is set at the factory on a special testing device. In the field, without the proper equipment, the spring pressure cannot be accurately reset, so the best that can be done is to put it back where it was.

On other injectors the opening-spring pressure is set by fitting a number of shims (spacers) under the spring. The more shims, the higher the opening pressure. Every 0.001″ (one thousandths of an inch) increase in shim thickness raises the opening pressure by about 55 psi. These injectors have no external spring adjustment, and you can move directly to removal of the nozzle assembly.

Now, unscrew the injector nozzle nut. Some injectors are designed to project a spray in a specific direction. In this case, the nozzle and injector body are held in the correct relationship with a small dowel. If the nozzle nut is particularly hard to break loose, the whole assembly should be soaked again because excessive force is likely to damage the dowel pin. Sometimes a sharp tap on the end of the wrench is necessary to break the grip of carbon in the injector and get the nozzle nut moving. Once the nozzle nut is off, the nozzle and its components can be removed. The order of all the parts must be carefully noted. *On no account must injectors be mixed up*—the nozzles and needle valves are machined as matching sets and a particular pair must always go together.

All contact surfaces within the injector should be clean and bright. The caustic soda solution, appropriate scrapers, or both are

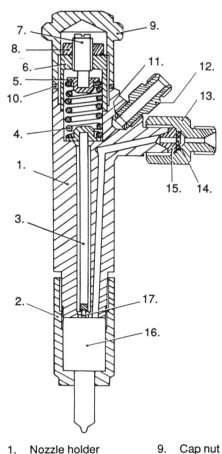

1. Nozzle holder
2. Nozzle nut
3. Spindle
4. Spring
5. Upper spring plate
6. Spring cap nut
7. Spring adjusting screw
8. Locknut
9. Cap nut
10. Joint washer
11. Joint washer
12. Leak-off adaptor
13. Inlet adaptor
14. Filter
15. Nipple
16. Nozzle
17. Needle

Figure 12-12. *Injector with spring adjusting screw. (Courtesy Lucas CAV Ltd.)*

used to clean up any carbon inside the injector. Take care not to scratch the needle valve, its seat, or the nozzle bore. *No abrasive cleaning or grinding compounds should ever be used on the needle or its seat in the nozzle. These are machined at different angles to ensure a tight line contact (see Figure 12-13). Any grinding or lapping will destroy this fit.*

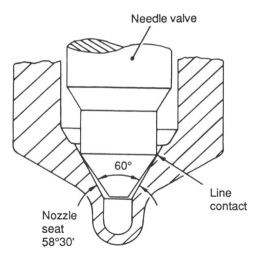

Figure 12-13. *Angular difference between nozzle seat and needle valve (multi-hole injector). (Courtesy Lucas CAV Ltd.)*

Injector manufacturers sell nozzle cleaning kits (see Figure 12-16). The following are the instructions issued by CAV on the use of their kit (CAV workshop manual #C/P 24E "Fuel Injectors", page 7):

"To clean the nozzle of a multihole injector with the tool kit:

1. Remove all traces of carbon deposit from the exterior of the nozzle (A) (refer back to Figure 12-12) and from the needle (B) with the wire brush (7). Polish the needle with a piece of soft wood; do not use an abrasive cleaning compound.

2. Clean the gallery (E) with the scraper (1).

3. Clean the nozzle seat (G) with the

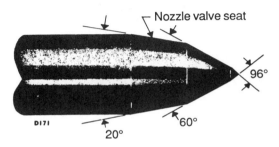

Figure 12-14. *Nozzle valve seat. (Courtesy United Technologies Diesel Systems.)*

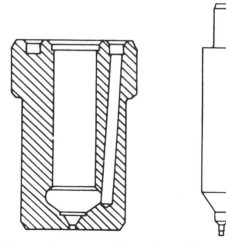

Figure 12-15. *Nozzle and needle (pintle). (Courtesy Lucas CAV Ltd.)*

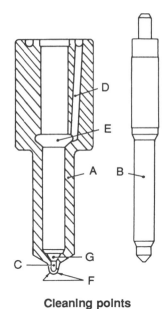

Cleaning points

A. Nozzle	E. Gallery
B. Needle	F. Spray holes
C. Cavity	G. Nozzle seat
D. Feed hole	

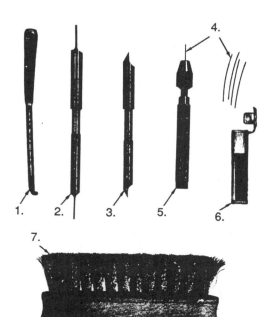

Nozzle cleaning kit

1. Scraper (gallery)
2. Scraper (cavity)
3. Scraper (nozzle seat)
4. Pricker wires
5. Pin vice for pricker wires
6. Container (pricker wires)
7. Brass wire brush

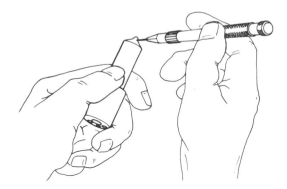

Clear spray holes by use of the probing tool fitted with 0.38 mm diameter cleaning wire. Fit the wire in the chuck so it protrudes only about 1.5 mm, giving maximum resistance to bending. Enter wire into each hole, pushing and rotating gently until each hole is cleared. Note: different nozzles will need different sizes of cleaning wire.

Figure 12-16. *Cleaning the nozzle and needle. (Courtesy Lucas CAV Ltd.)*

scraper (3), using the appropriate end of the scraper.

4. Similarly, clean the cavity (C) with the scraper (2).

5. Use the pin vise (5) with the appropriate size of pricker wire (4) to clean the spray holes (F) in the nozzle tip. The pin vise must be used carefully to avoid the risk of breaking the pricker wire in a spray hole.''

A clean needle valve should drop easily onto its seat and fall back out when the injector is inverted. Injector parts must be spotlessly clean (lint-free rags only) and then dipped in clean diesel before reassembly.

Reassembly of an injector is a reversal of the disassembly procedure. All kinds of things should be checked, such as nozzle lift and spring pressures, but these are beyond the scope of an amateur mechanic. (That is why—if at all possible—injectors should be left alone!) The opening pressure adjusting screw (if fitted) should be screwed back down to its previous position, as already noted. All shims must be put back exactly as before, in the same order with a thick spacer on the top and bottom of the thin spacers. The spray pattern can then be checked again.

If the spring setting has been lost on an adjustable spring, the adjusting screw should be turned down until it is finger tight. Thereafter every turn represents 900–1,000 psi opening spring pressure. Multihole injectors are generally set to around 2,200 psi (2–2½ more turns), and pintle nozzles to around 1,500 psi (1½ turns). If the spray pattern is still poor, it may be improved by tightening the spring pressure by up to ¾ of a turn more, but certainly no more than this. If after all this the needle valve fails to seat properly and the injector refuses to operate correctly, you can do nothing short of replacing the nozzle and needle valve assembly—or the whole injector.

It is essential that an injector make a gas-tight seal in its cylinder head. The hole in the head must be clean; a new sealing washer (if one is used) should be fitted if at all possible. If the injector is of the type held down with a steel plate it must be squarely seated and the hold-down bolts evenly torqued. A smear of high-temperature grease around the injector barrel will prevent corrosion from locking it in the cylinder head.

Fuel lines are specifically made for individual cylinders, and must be returned to these cylinders. The lines will make an exact fit: both ends should be put in place at the same time and then both hand-tightened before final tightening. No bending or forcing to fit should ever be needed.

If fuel nuts are overtightened, the sealing nipples will probably be irreparably damaged. If a fuel line needs replacing, *the correct individual line* must be bought from the engine manufacturer. A fuel pipe of the wrong length will throw out the fuel timing by a very small amount because there is a minute time lag between the injection pump stroking and the fuel's injection—the longer the pipe, the longer the time lag. This is taken into account when the engine is first designed, and the fuel lines are made to the appropriate length.

Annealing washers

Injectors are often sealed in cylinder heads with copper washers. In time, and after being subjected to high temperatures, these washers become hard and lose their sealing properties. Copper can easily be softened again by heating it with a propane torch (or primus, or whatever) until it is a cherry-red color and then dropping it into cold water. This is known as *annealing*. (For some reason copper-based metals are annealed by rapid cooling, whereas iron-based metals are annealed by slow cooling—rapid cooling of iron induces hardness.)

Gaskets

Sometimes it is necessary to improvise a gasket in the field. Your repair kit should contain a roll of high-temperature gasket material, plus some cork or rubber-based material for valve cover and pan (sump) gaskets. Most other gaskets can be made from brown paper, if necessary, using several layers.

Even complicated gaskets are relatively simple to make. The trick is to lay a sheet of gasket material over the piece that needs the gasket. Using the ball end of a ball peen hammer (see Figure 12-17), the gasket should be tapped lightly into all the bolt holes. The relatively sharp edges of the bolt holes will cut the gasket, enabling a perfect hole to be made. A bolt is slipped through the gasket to hold it to the piece at this point. This procedure is repeated at a couple more widely spaced bolt holes, and the sheet of gasket paper will now be held securely in place. Tap out any holes or other areas that need to be cut out of the gasket until it is complete. The keys to success are striking the gasket in a way that forces it against the sharpest edge of the piece being gasketed; and using the minimum necessary force (especially on aluminum) to avoid damage (burred edges, cracked castings, etc.). A flurry of light taps is far better than a heavy blow.

If you don't have a ball peen hammer, a box-end wrench or any other curved metal object can be used. Where the outline of the piece being gasketed is not sharp enough to cut the gasket paper, an oily finger rubbed over it will leave a clear enough line to be followed by a knife or pair of scissors.

Electrical equipment

Batteries. Batteries need little more than to be kept topped up, charged, and clean (especially the terminals). If a battery becomes fully discharged and is then recharged (this is known as *deep cycling*), it suffers some internal damage. A battery can only be deep cycled so many times before it is destroyed—the number of times varies from battery to battery. The tendency to anchor up somewhere and run the ship's battery all the way down before cranking up the engine (on a separate battery) and recharging should be avoided. This is guaranteed to shorten battery life.

A battery standing idle will slowly discharge itself, especially at warmer temperatures (at 100°F it will lose as much as 3% of its charge *every day*). If a boat is laid up for more than a month, the battery should be kept on charge or periodically recharged, or it will deep cycle without any help from its owner.

The only effective way to check the state of charge of a battery is with a hydrometer. A hydrometer has a float, weighted on its bottom end, and a scale on its side. In pure water the float will read 1.00 on the scale—this is known as the specific gravity of water.

A fully charged battery contains a solution of sulphuric acid, which is denser than water; therefore, a hydrometer will float

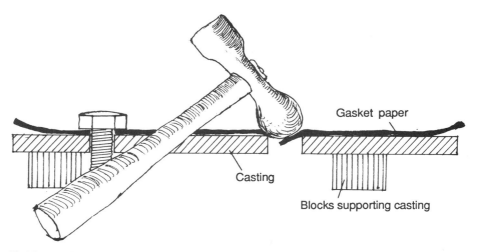

Gasket paper

Casting

Blocks supporting casting

Figure 12-17. *Making a gasket.*

higher in this liquid. As the battery discharges, the sulphuric acid turns to water and the hydrometer sinks lower. A fully charged battery will read around 1.280 on a hydrometer scale at 60 °F (a little lower in warmer weather). A partially discharged battery reads around 1.200, and a discharged battery around 1.115.

Each cell must be tested individually. A battery may have five good cells and one dead one, and a battery is only as good as its weakest cell. Once a battery refuses to hold its charge, you must replace it.

Alternators. Alternators produce alternating current (AC), while batteries produce direct current (DC). In order to make the two compatible, the output from the alternator is rectified by diodes. If the alternator circuit to the battery is broken at any time while the alternator is running, the build-up of electricity in the alternator will rapidly burn out the diodes, frequently in a matter of seconds. At the very least this necessitates a new rectifier and voltage regulator, and normally a new alternator as well, since these items are built into many alternators.

Most boats are fitted with a battery isolation switch. If this switch is opened (the batteries isolated) while the engine is running, the engine will continue to run (remember diesels require no electronic ignition), and the alternator will burn out in no time at all.

The most common cause of poor or no charging is a broken or slipping drive belt. Alternators can put a considerable load on an engine (up to several horsepower), so drive belts should be checked regularly and kept tight. It should not be possible to depress the longest stretch of belt by more than ½ ″ with your finger.

Starter motors. Starter motors are remarkably reliable and generally give advance notice of impending trouble through sluggish action, failure to cleanly engage the starting ring on the flywheel, grinding, and whirring noises, etc. Although it is possible to carry a spare solenoid or Bendix unit (the spring-loaded gear that engages the flywheel) and to change these if necessary, it makes more sense to nip trouble in the bud and to install a reconditioned starter at the first sign of a problem.

Because of the high amperage and heavy cables needed to start an internal-combustion engine, the starting circuit is not run through the ignition switch. Instead the cables are run to a separate switch, a solenoid, mounted on the starter motor or close to it. This switch is then connected to the ignition switch.

A solenoid is an electromagnet. When the ignition switch is turned on the magnet is energized and pulls two heavy-duty contacts together, which allows the full battery current to flow to the starter motor.

Starter motors are of two basic kinds: *inertia* and *pre-engaged*. A solenoid of an inertia starter motor is generally mounted at an independent, convenient location. The starter motor drive gear is keyed into a helical groove on its drive shaft. When the solenoid is energized the starter spins, and the inertia of the gear causes it to fly out along the helical groove to engage the engine flywheel, which is then turned over.

The solenoid of a pre-engaged starter is mounted on the starter itself. When the solenoid is energized, the electromagnet first pulls a lever that pushes the starter motor drive gear into engagement with the engine flywheel, and then closes the contacts to the starter motor, causing it to spin. Thus, the drive gear is meshed with the flywheel *before* the motor starts to spin, which greatly reduces overall wear.

If the battery is fully charged but the starter motor fails to spin when the ignition key is turned, and you can hear a clicking noise from the solenoid, then the starter motor is probably faulty. In the absence of a clicking noise the solenoid itself may be giving trouble—the circuit to the ignition switch is bad, the electromagnet is burned up, or the heavy-duty main contacts are burned and corroded. A few simple tests will determine where the fault lies.

The ignition circuit comprises two smaller wires entering the solenoid, one being connected to the same terminal as the main supply cable from the battery, and the other to a smaller terminal nearby. The ignition switch can be bypassed by connecting a jumper wire across these two terminals; if this causes the starter to work, there is a problem in the wiring to the ignition switch or in the switch itself.

There is another possibility for inertia starters. There will be a battery cable going into the starter and another going out, and if a screwdriver is used to jump these two terminals the solenoid will be bypassed altogether. If the starter now works, the solenoid needs replacing. It should be noted that the full starting current of the battery will be flowing through the screwdriver blade; it will have to be held very firmly across the two terminals or considerable arcing will occur, and enough heat can be generated to melt a big chunk of the blade! Obviously, anytime you knowingly create a spark, the engine room should first be well ventilated (especially with gasoline engines) and a check made for any combustibles (particularly fuel in the bilges and leaking propane stoves). Repeated jumping out of a solenoid in this fashion is likely to lead to battery and starter damage.

A pre-engaged starter cannot be jumped out in this fashion. If the solenoid is completely bypassed the motor will spin, but the starter drive gear will not be pushed into the flywheel and the engine will not turn over. One can at least determine whether it is the solenoid or starter motor that is defective, however. If the starter spins, the solenoid is bad.

Oil and filter changes

Many marine engines have a sump pump installed, which enables the oil to be pumped out manually at oil change time. This is important because generally the pan (sump) drain plug is inaccessible. If no pump is fitted, you may slide a piece of tubing into the dipstick hole, attach a hand pump to it, and pump out the oil this way.

Oil should be changed when the engine is at normal operating temperature. The hot oil is much thinner and will drain down freely

from the various engine passages. Oil and fuel filters are now almost always of the spin-on variety, and changing one is simplicity itself. Bear in mind the following points:

1. All external dirt should be cleaned off the filter housing before the old filter is removed.
2. If a filter will not unscrew, generally a screwdriver or spike driven through its side will provide enough leverage to get it started.
3. If the new filter has its own sealing ring, it is important to ensure that the old one does not remain stuck to the filter housing. If the new filter has no sealing ring, then you'll have to reuse the old one, but in this case a stock of spare rings should be bought and a new one fitted at each oil change.
4. If a new fuel filter is filled with diesel before installation it will reduce the amount of priming that must be done.
5. Filters are screwed on hand tight and then given an additional three-quarters of a turn, or so. They should not be overtightened.

Governors

On occasion, a governor will fail to hold a set speed, particularly on start-up. The engine continually speeds up and then slows down rhythmically. This is known as *hunting*. Although various engine malfunctions, such as misfiring or poor injection, may contribute to it, most likely some part of the governor mechanism or fuel injection pump control linkage is sticking. The governor then has to overreact to any change in load in order to overcome resistance to movement of the fuel-control rod. Then the rod moves with a jerk and goes too far, causing the engine to overspeed or underspeed. The governor then overreacts once again, but in the other direction, and the engine underspeeds or overspeeds, and so on. Excessive slack or play in the fuel pump control linkage (throttle linkage) will cause a similar symptom.

By-passing the ignition switch by jumping out the two smaller wires.

By-passing the solenoid altogether by jumping out the two main cable terminals.

Figure 12-18. *Jumping out a solenoid.*

If the governor is inside the engine (as opposed to the fuel injection pump), the governor mechanism itself may be giving rise to the problem. In this case it is quite likely that a build-up of sludge from a failure to carry out adequate engine oil changes is interfering with correct governor operation. You will have to get at and clean the governor.

The only other likely maintenance on the governor is an occasional adjustment of the idle setting on the speeder spring. There is normally no cause to alter this. If the engine will not idle correctly it is almost certainly due to some other problem. The idle setting should only be adjusted *when the engine is*

running well. Engine-mounted governors have a screw and locknut somewhere on the outside of the block. Governors inside injection pumps generally have an external low-speed screw acting directly on the throttle control lever.

Somewhere there will also be a maximum fuel setting screw and locknut that will almost certainly be tied off with lockwire and sealed. *Do not tamper with it.* If the seal is broken, it automatically voids any engine warranty. Should it not be sealed, and if the engine appears to be overloaded at full throttle (making black smoke, overheating) the maximum fuel setting should be reduced. *Increasing maximum fuel settings above manufacturers' set points can lead to engine seizure.*

Governor control lever (throttle)   Idle speed fuel setting screw

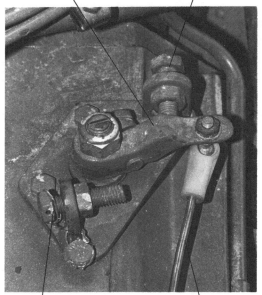

Maximum fuel screw with lockwire and seal   Throttle (governor control) linkage

Figure 12-19. *Maximum fuel setting screw on a Volvo MD 17C.*

Air out

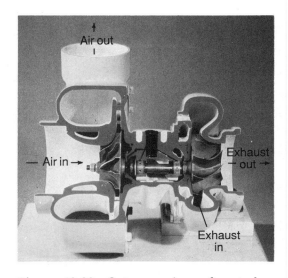

Air in →   Exhaust out →

Exhaust in

Figure 12-20. *Cutaway view of a turbocharger. (Courtesy Caterpillar Tractor Co.)*

Turbochargers

WARNING: Turbochargers operate at high speeds and temperatures. One must keep fingers away from openings and avoid contact with hot surfaces. A turbocharger should never be operated without all normal filters and ducting in place.

Turbochargers turn at up to 120,000 r.p.m. Their bearings float in a film of oil, and it is absolutely critical to long life that this oil be clean and maintained at a good pressure. Turbochargers are one of the first things to suffer from poor oil-change procedures.

A turbocharged engine should never be raced immediately after start-up, for one must allow time for oil to be pumped to the bearings. Similarly, the engine should never be revved up before shutting down, since the finely balanced turbines will continue to spin for some time without the benefit of oil pumped to the bearings. (As a general rule, no diesel engine should be revved up and down—it creates undue stresses that are bound to shorten engine life.)

The degree of precision required in modern turbochargers means that they should be rebuilt only by professionals, but before calling in the experts you can make a few checks to ensure that the turbocharger itself is defective. The following procedure is adapted, with thanks, from material supplied by the Garrett Automotive Products Company:

1. Start the engine and *listen*. If a turbocharger is cycling up and down in pitch there is probably a restriction in the air inlet (most likely a clogged filter). A whistling sound is quite likely caused by a leak in the inlet or exhaust piping.

2. Stop the engine and remove the inlet and exhaust pipes from the turbine housings. (These are the pipes going into the *center* of the turbine housings.) This will give a view of the turbine wheels. With a flashlight, check for chipped or bent blades, rub marks on the wheels or housings, excessive dirt on the wheels, or oil in the housings. The latter

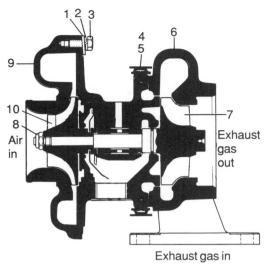

1. Washer
2. Lock washer
3. Bolts fastening
   compressor cover
4. V-clamp
5. V-clamp lock nut
6. Turbine housing
7. Exhaust turbine
8. Main shaft nut
9. Compressor housing
10. Compressor turbine

Figure 12-21. *Holset 3LD/3LE Turbo-charger. (Courtesy Holset Engineering Co. Ltd.)*

symptom may indicate oil seal failure, but before assuming this one should check for other possible sources.

3. Push in on the wheels and turn them to feel for any rubbing or binding. Try this from both sides.

If these tests reveal no problems, the turbocharger is probably OK. If it failed on any count (except dirty turbine blades) it should be removed as a unit and sent to a specialist.

Should the turbines need cleaning, the housings can be removed to give access to the blades. First, however, mark both housings and the center unit with scribed lines so that they can be reassembled in the identical relationship to one another. The hous-

ings are held on with bolts, large clamps, or snap rings. Some bolts have locking tabs that will need straightening before the bolts can be undone. If the housings are held on with snap rings, the turbochargers will disassemble readily but will require a hydraulic press and special tools to go back together again. To take apart such a turbocharger, identify each snap ring in such a way that it can be put back in the same position on the same housing.

If the housings are difficult to break loose, they should be tapped with a soft hammer or mallet. To remove the housings, lift them clear squarely to avoid bending any turbine blades. Turbines should be cleaned with *noncaustic* solutions (de-greasers work well) using a soft bristle brush and plastic scrapers. No abrasives should be used, because any damage to the blades will upset the critical balance of the turbines. Do not attempt to straighten bent blades; if this misfortune occurs, the turbine must be replaced.

Dismantling the center unit is not recommended. If you do attempt it for any reasons, note that the center retaining nut has a *left-hand thread*.

The procedure for reassembly is the reverse of disassembly. Be sure to line up all scribed marks accurately, and when you are done, spin the turbines by hand to make sure they turn freely. After a turbocharger is serviced, the engine should be cranked over for

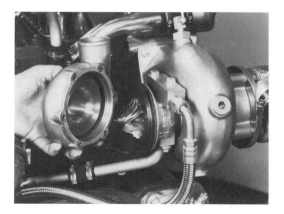

Figure 12-22. *Removing a turbocharger housing. (Courtesy Perkins Engines Ltd.)*

a while before it is started to circulate oil through the turbocharger bearings.

Winterizing

Certain aspects of laying up a boat for the winter have already been covered. Here is a quick recapitulation and a couple of additional points.

1. All raw-water systems must be drained, with particular attention to low spots. On engines with raw-water-cooled exhausts, it is a good idea to close the intake seacock and then to run the engine for a moment or two to drive the water out of the exhaust system.
2. The antifreeze should be checked in closed cooling systems and preferably renewed.
3. The battery should be removed from the boat and put on charge.
4. The primary fuel filter sediment bowl should be checked for any water, and a sample taken from the tank, which should be pumped out as necessary. The tank should be filled to reduce the volume of air, which will cut down on condensation.
5. *The engine oil should be changed at the beginning of the winter and not the end.* Diesel engine oils build up corrosive acids and some water over time. You do not want these going to work on the bearings all winter long.
6. A few squirts of oil should be put in the air inlet manifold if at all possible and the engine turned over to draw it into the cylinders and spread it around the upper cylinder walls.
7. All grease points should be greased.

Chapter Thirteen

Marine Gearboxes

Three types of gearbox are in common use on small marine engines:
1. manual planetary, the original marine boxes now generally only found on older engines;
2. two-shaft manual boxes;
3. hydraulic boxes, the almost universal choice for today's engines.

Manual planetary *(epicyclic)* boxes

The drive shaft from the engine on a planetary box has a gear that drives two pinion gears, which drive two more spur gears, themselves enclosed in a geared band. The pinion and spur gears are mounted on a common assembly that is free to rotate around the drive gear. If the drive gear, pinion gears, spur gears, and geared band are locked up as a single unit, then they all will rotate together in the same direction of rotation as the engine. This is what happens when the gearbox is in forward gear.

If the outer geared band is locked in one position, when the center shaft turns one way (driven by the engine) the pinion gears will rotate in the opposite direction. The spur gears turn in the same direction as the drive gear, which causes the pinion and spur gear assembly to rotate inside the geared band in the opposite direction to the drive gear (Figure 13-1). The pinion and spur gear

assembly is connected to the output shaft, giving reverse gear.

This is the principle of a planetary gearbox. For forward, the gears are locked up with the propeller shaft by a clutch in such a way that the whole assembly rotates as one unit. In reverse, a brake band is clamped around the large outer geared band, causing the inner gears to rotate around the inner drive gear, but in the opposite direction, and this rotation is transmitted to the propeller shaft.

The two key components in a planetary box that need regular attention are the adjustments of the clutch and the brake band. Different manufacturers have different adjustment points, but in general these boxes have large covers that provide access to the whole insides, and if the cover is removed and the gears operated a few times, the adjustment points will become evident. Clutches normally have from three to six tensioning nuts. They should be tightened no more than one-sixth of a turn at one time, and they need to be tightened evenly. Brake bands generally have some kind of a central clamping device. After adjustment the gear lever should be operated and checked for a firm feel and positive engagement of the gears.

Clutch plates and brake bands eventually will wear enough to cause the gear box to jump out of gear or slip under load. Slipping

FORWARD GEAR

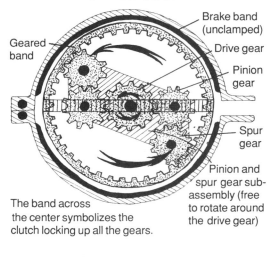

The band across the center symbolizes the clutch locking up all the gears.

REVERSE GEAR

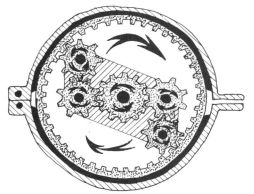

The brake band is clamped down, locking up the geared band. The pinion and spur gear sub-assembly is driven around the band in the opposite direction to the drive gear.

Figure 13-1. *An epicyclic gearbox.*

will rapidly heat up the gearbox and lead to more serious trouble. Once this point is reached, you have to renew clutch plates and brake bands, for which a manufacturer's manual will be required.

Two-shaft manual gearboxes

Planetary gearboxes suffer from two disadvantages: a large number of moving parts, and the power losses attendant in turning all these parts. A two-shaft gearbox reduces both problems. The engine drive shaft has two gears on it, spaced apart. A second shaft has two gears on it, one directly engaging one of the gears on the drive shaft, the other engaging the second gear on the drive shaft via an intermediate gear. The second shaft has a clutch for each gear (see Figure 13-2).

If the clutch on the gear directly locked to the engine drive shaft is engaged, reverse rotation is imparted to the output shaft. If the clutch on the gear with an intermediate gear is engaged, the same rotation is imparted to the output shaft (see Figure 13-2).

By varying the sizes of the various gears, any degree of engine reduction can be built into this assembly. The clutches are the only owner-adjustable components and the same comments made about planetary clutches apply. Some boxes have cone-type clutches, which operate on the principle that once an initial engagement is made, the propeller thrust pushes the output shaft (in forward) or pulls it (in reverse) into the clutch assembly, completing clutch operation. Cone clutches have no adjustment. When they start to slip they must be replaced. Good propeller alignment (see Chapter 14) is essential with cone clutches in order to exert an even pressure on the clutch.

Hydraulic gearboxes

Most hydraulic gearboxes operate on the same principle as manual planetary boxes, but instead of manual gear shifting a hydraulic gearbox contains an oil pump, and oil pressure is used to operate the forward and reverse gears. It is therefore very easy to fit remote controls, and gear shifting is a fingertip affair. Hydraulic gearboxes are remarkably reliable, which is just as well because there are really no user-adjustable or serviceable parts. The only thing that should be checked once in a while (apart from oil levels, of course) is that the remote control has a free and easy movement and that the neutral position on the control actually corresponds to the neutral position on the gearbox selector. Figure 13-3 illustrates two

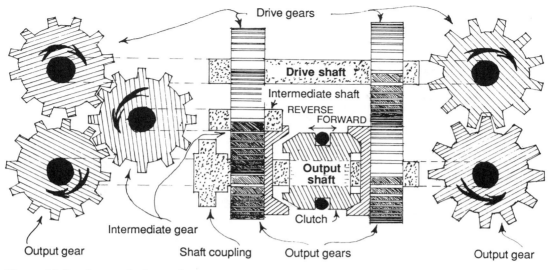

Figure 13-2. *A two-shaft gearbox.*

hydraulic boxes manufactured by Borg-Warner.

The following problems with hydraulic boxes are relatively easy to identify and fix.

1. No forward or reverse. The oil level should be checked and the oil topped up if necessary. Low oil will sometimes cause air to be sucked into the hydraulic circuit, which will cause a buzzing noise—topping up and running the engine in neutral will clear out the air. If the boat still has no forward or reverse, *before assuming the gearbox is at fault the output coupling should be checked to see if it is turning.* If the coupling is spinning, the problem may be that the propeller shaft coupling is slipping on its shaft; the coupling bolts are missing or sheared; the propeller itself is missing or damaged; or the propeller may simply be cavitating and transmitting no drive to the boat (see the next chapter).

2. Improper operation of either forward or reverse. Before you assume that there are serious problems, *the gear shift lever on the side of the gearbox should be checked to see that it is in the right position.*

3. Overheating. Most hydraulic gearboxes have oil coolers—heat exchangers which utilize the engine cooling water to cool the gearbox oil. The most likely cause of gearbox overheating is a failure of the cooling circuit for any of the reasons outlined in Chapter 12. Far less likely is an obstruction in the oil side of the cooler or oil lines.

A sailboat owner occasionally will freewheel the propeller when the boat is under sail and use the spinning propeller shaft to drive an alternator for battery charging. However, on some (but not all) hydraulic gearboxes this will lead to bearing failure through lack of lubrication. On these boxes the shaft has to be locked in place when the engine is not in use.

Gearboxes and reduction gears come as *in-line, offset* or *V-drive*. In-line simply means that the output flange is in the same plane (i.e. at the same height) as the input shaft to the box. Offset boxes have the output shaft lower than, or set to one side of, the input shaft. V-drives are illustrated in Figure 13-3. The extra gearing absorbs some power, but sometimes a V-drive is the only way to get an engine into a tight corner, or to keep the engine weight well to the rear of the planing sport fishing boat (see Chapter 15)

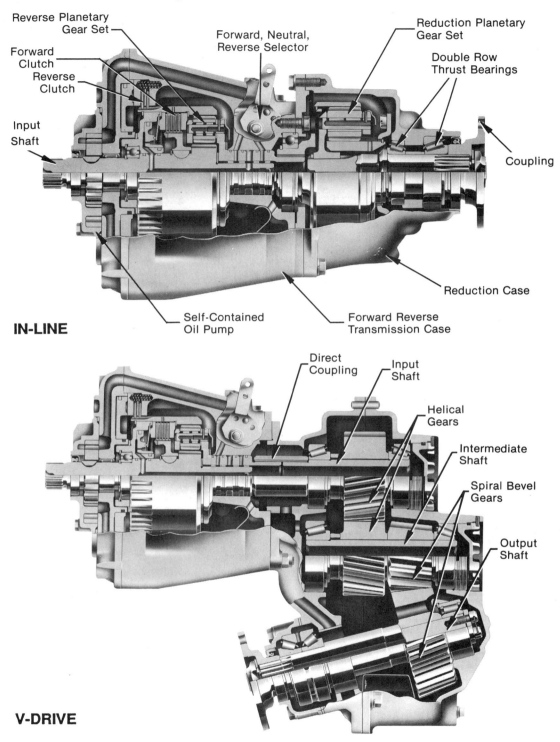

Figure 13-3. *In-line and V-drive hydraulic gearboxes. (Courtesy Borg-Warner.)*

for more discussion of weight distribution in this type of boat).

Inboard/outboards

As more and more diesels find their way into sporting boats, inboard/outboard transmissions are beginning to get coupled up to them and so deserve a brief mention.

Inboard/outboards are exactly what their name implies—an inboard engine coupled to an outboard-motor-type drive assembly and propeller arrangement (see Figure 13-4). These units have definite advantages in planing pleasure craft, notably:

1. Inboard/outboards allow an engine to be mounted in the stern of a boat, which is the best place in terms of weight distribution on many planing hulls.
2. The outboard unit can be hydraulically pivoted up and down. This enables these boats to take full advantage of their shallow draft to run up on beaches, makes trailering easy, and provides infinite propeller depth adjustment for changes in boat trim.
3. The whole outboard unit turns for steering, greatly increasing maneuverability and removing the need for a separate rudder installation.
4. There is no propeller shaft, stern tube, or stuffing box to leak into the boat.

All the extra gearing and the sharp changes in drive angle, however, absorb power. For this reason inboard/outboard use is generally limited very specifically to planing pleasure craft.

Gearbox oil seals

In the days of plank-on-frame boats it was not uncommon to have bilge water slopping around the gearbox and up the back of the output-shaft oil seal. In time, as seals weakened, there would be a loss of lubricating oil into the bilges and water penetration into the gearbox. This is no longer a common problem, but nevertheless the seals need

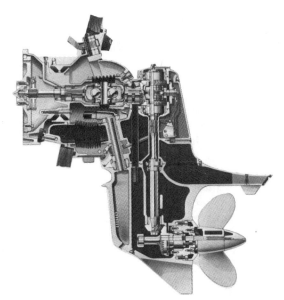

Figure 13-4. *An inboard/outboard. (Courtesy Volvo Penta.)*

to be checked for oil leakage from time to time. Vibration from a misaligned propeller shaft or incorrectly mounted auxiliary equipment (see Chapter 14) can knock out a rear seal quite rapidly. In fact, an oil leak out of the transmission is often the first sign of misalignment.

Some seals are easier to change than others, depending on the layout of the gearbox housing and propeller shaft. The first step is to unbolt and separate the two halves of the propeller coupling. It is a good practice to mark both halves so that they can be bolted back together in the same relation to one another.

Next the coupling half attached to the gearbox output shaft must be removed. This coupling is held in place with a central nut. On most modern boxes the nut is done up tightly, but on some older boxes it is just pinched up and then locked in place with a cotter key. It is essential that the latter type be replaced in a similar fashion—the best thing is to pull them up to a moderate tightness to make sure everything is properly seated, and then to back off an eighth of a turn or so before inserting the cotter key. The box should then be put in neutral and the coupling turned by hand to make sure that there is no binding.

The gearbox output coupling is either on a splined shaft (one with ridges along it all the way around) or a keyed shaft (one with a single square locking bar inserted in a slot in the shaft and fitting into a slot in the coupling). In the latter case, care must be taken when removing the coupling not to lose the key down in the bilges. What is more likely, however, is that the key will stick in the shaft. If there is no risk of its falling out and getting lost it can be left there, but otherwise a screwdriver should be held up against one end and gently tapped until the end can be pried up and the key removed.

It's worth noting that on some boats with vertical rudder posts the propeller shaft cannot be pushed back far enough to provide the necessary room to slide the gearbox coupling off its shaft! What happens is that the propeller hits the rudder stock and will go no further. In this case the rudder has to be removed or the engine lifted off its mounts to provide the necessary space. This is an awful lot of work to change an oil seal. (In such a case, you may want to consider having the propeller shaft shortened and installing a small stub shaft in line between the gearbox and propeller shaft.)

Gearbox oil seals are a press fit into the rear gearbox housing. Seals are made with a rubber-coated steel case with a flat face on the rear end and a rubber lip on the front end (the end inside the gearbox). Inside a seal is a spring which holds this lip against the coupling face to be sealed.

Removing a seal from its housing is not easy. If at all possible, the housing should be unbolted from the gearbox and taken to a convenient workbench. (This is often fairly simple on older boxes and reduction gears but may not be feasible on many modern hydraulic boxes.) The seal may be dug out with chisels, screwdrivers, steel hooks, or any other implement that comes to hand—it doesn't matter if the seal gets chewed up *so long as the housing and shaft (if still in place) are unscratched.*

New seals are placed into a housing with

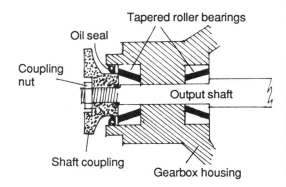

Figure 13.5 *Typical thrust-bearing arrangement and location of engine gearbox oil seal.*

the rubber lip facing *into* the gearbox, and the flat face outside. It is critical to place a seal in *squarely* and then to tap it in evenly using a block of wood and a hammer. *If a seal is forced in cock-eyed it will be damaged.* The block of wood is necessary to maintain an even pressure over the whole seal face—*a seal should never be hit directly as it will distort.* A seal is pushed in until the rear end is flush with the face of the gearbox housing. Once in place some seals will require greasing (there will be a grease fitting on the back of the gearbox) but most need no further attention.

Reassembly of a coupling and propeller shaft is a reversal of disassembly. Propeller shaft alignment should be checked anytime

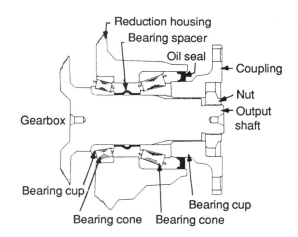

Figure 13-6. *Pre-loaded thrust bearings.*

the coupling halves are broken loose and done back up (see next chapter).

Many gearboxes with tightly done up coupling nuts have what are called "preloaded" thrust bearings. The gearbox output shaft, on which the coupling is mounted, turns in two sets of tapered roller bearings— one facing in each direction. Between the two is a steel sleeve. When the coupling nut is pulled up this sleeve is compressed, maintaining tension on the bearings and eliminating any play (see Figure 13-6).

Anytime the coupling nut is undone, a torque wrench should be used and the pressure needed to break the nut loose noted. When the nut is done back up, it should be pulled up to the same torque *plus 2-5 ft. lbs.* in order to maintain the correct bearing preloading. In any event, the torque should be at least 160 ft. lbs. on most Borg-Warner boxes, but the coupling should still turn freely by hand with only minimal drag. Should a new bearing spacer be fitted between the thrust bearings, a special jig and procedure is called for and the whole gearbox reduction unit will have to go to a professional.

Chapter Fourteen

Engine Installations

This chapter may seem to be of little relevance to those who already have an engine installed in their boat, but frequently enough engine problems arise from inadequate or improper installation, and these pages may throw some light on a long-standing problem.

Ventilation

A diesel engine requires a large volume of clean air (as already shown in Chapter 8), at a cool temperature. As air temperatures rise, the *weight* of air per cubic foot falls and the engine pulls in correspondingly less oxygen at each inlet stroke, with a resulting loss in efficiency and power.

Figure 14-1 gives an approximate idea of the decrease in the weight of air as temperatures rise. It is not uncommon for engine rooms in the tropics to be as hot as 120°F, with turbocharging air inlet temperatures considerably higher. In excessively hot engine rooms it will be necessary to duct air in from the outside directly to the inlet manifold. If such ducting is installed, its opening must be situated in such a way that water cannot enter it, and as far from the exhaust as possible so that the spent gases are not sucked back into the engine. Figure 14-2 shows the decrease in engine rated output as inlet air temperatures rise (as determined by the

Diesel Engine Manufacturers Association—the rating starts at 90°F.

Fuel supply

The density of diesel also decreases with rising temperatures. Fuel temperatures above 90°F will result in reduced engine power. The higher the fuel tank in an engine room, the warmer the fuel will get, and so it is advisable to keep tanks down low. In any event, the top of the tank should not be above the level of the injectors because occasionally it is possible for fuel to leak down through the injectors into the combustion chambers. A low tank will also help to provide stability to the boat. Centrally placed tanks will not affect athwartships trim.

The distance from the bottom of a fuel tank to the fuel lift pump should be measured and compared to the lifting capacity of the pump. An auxiliary lift pump may be needed in certain exceptional cases.

Fuel tanks can be made of fiberglass, epoxied or glass-covered wood, plain (black) steel, or aluminum, but NOT galvanized steel. *The fuel system should not have galvanized steel anywhere in it.* The zinc in galvanizing is dissolved by sulfur traces in the diesel and forms a sludge that will plug up injectors and harm the engine. Tanks should be baffled at regular intervals in order to

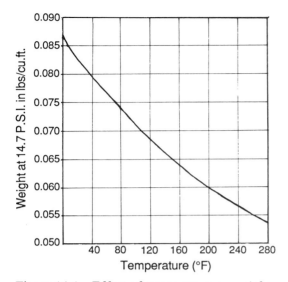

Figure 14-1. *Effect of temperature on weight of air.*

prevent the fuel from sloshing around—no compartment should exceed twenty-five gallons. If the fuel does slosh around, it will become aerated and cause problems with the fuel injection system.

However much care is taken in filtering fuel, sooner or later all tanks need cleaning. Every compartment in a fuel tank needs a

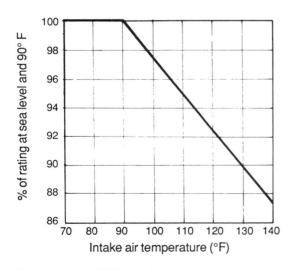

Figure 14-2. *Effect of air temperature on diesel engine performance.*

generous access hatch. It is an excellent idea, if feasible, to fit a small sump at the lowest point of the tank with either an accessible drain or some provision to pump out this sump. This greatly helps routine removal of water and sediment from the tank.

In general, it is a good idea to have all fuel lines, drain lines, and so on coming out of the top of the tank, and led down to the bottom as necessary. If a line should rupture it will not lead to the loss of all the diesel fuel into the bilges. In order to avoid picking up water and trash, the diesel suction should not reach all the way to the bottom of the tank. A small check valve in its foot will prevent the fuel lines from draining back to the tank when filters are changed, but any resistance created by the check valve will have to be figured into the maximum lift-pump capability mentioned above.

The injector leak-off (return) lines must go *directly to the fuel tank*. It is an unfortunately common practice to run them back into the secondary filter to avoid having to install additional fuel lines to the tank. This frequently leads to problems with air in the fuel system. Finally, metal fuel tanks have to be grounded to prevent any build-up of static electricity, as do deck fill fittings.

Figure 14-3 illustrates a proper fuel-tank installation.

Cooling system

Especially on sailboats, the raw-water intake must be set very low (down by the garboard) to avoid sucking in air and air-locking the cooling system when the boat is heeled over or punching into a head sea. All cooling water piping must be designed with two things in mind: elimination of air traps; and the ability to drain all low spots on raw-water cooling circuits.

Any raw-water circuit must have plenty of easily renewable zinc pencil anodes to guard against galvanic corrosion. Always remember that the raw-water circuit is below the waterline, and defective piping or improper connections can sink the boat.

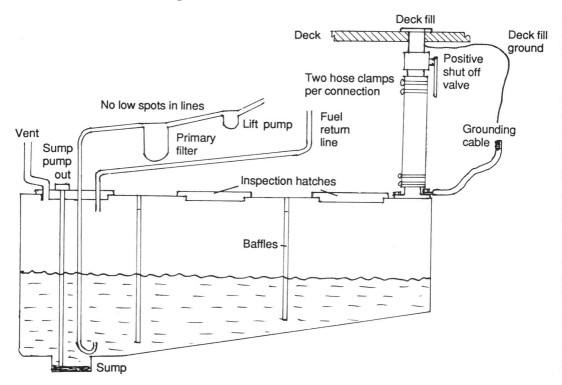

Figure 14-3. *A proper fuel-tank installation.*

Flexible connections

The fuel lines, cooling lines, and exhaust system all need flexible connections to the engine to handle engine vibration. These connections should be fastened with stainless steel hose clamps (including the screws, which frequently turn out to be cadmium plated and rust quickly). Use two clamps per connection for additional security. Only appropriate fuel lines and hoses should be used for these connections (i.e., fire resistant and in accordance with the relevant safety standards).

When you run fuel lines, take care to avoid high spots where pockets of air could gather. When you run water lines, you need to watch out for undrainable low spots where freezing might cause damage.

Exhausts

Exhaust installations need to be kept cool to keep down engine-room temperatures and to avoid burning engine operators or the bulkheads through which the exhaust passes. In general, dry exhausts will need insulating, while wet exhausts will run cool enough to pose no problems.

Exhaust back pressure has already been covered (Chapter 7). Suffice it to say that the exhaust pipe needs to be kept as short as possible, be of a large enough diameter and have as few bends as possible. It needs to terminate in a sea valve that is readily accessible so that when the engine is shut down, the exhaust can be positively closed off to keep following seas out. The higher the exhaust in the transom or stern of the boat, the less the risk of waves driving up it, and the easier it is to check the water flow out of a wet exhaust when the engine is running.

On sailboats, the exhaust is frequently some way under water when the boat is heeled, which considerably increases back pressure. The best kind of exhaust to deal with this situation is what has become known as the North Sea exhaust. Instead of the ex-

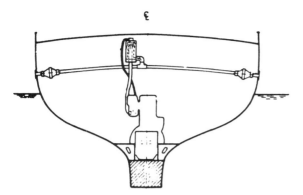

Figure 14-4. *North Sea exhaust (with alternative wet exhaust). (Courtesy Sabb Motor A.S.)*

haust pipe exiting through the transom, it is fed into a T and then exits on both sides of the hull (see Figure 14-4); in this design, one outlet is always above the water.

It is necessary to look in some detail at water-cooled exhausts, as incorrect installations can lead to water siphoning back into the engine and doing considerable damage. The two most common water-cooled systems are those of Onan and Vernalift, but numerous others are on the market. The idea is to spray raw water into the exhaust as it exits the engine, to have this water collect in the base of a silencer, and to then have it pushed out of the exhaust pipe by the exhaust gases.

The water-injection line needs to be angled down and away from the exhaust manifold to reduce the risk of water splashing back onto the exhaust valves and rusting them. Nevertheless, there is still a tendency for the valve nearest the exhaust outlet to rust—probably from steam coming back up the exhaust pipe after the engine is shut down.

The water-injection point must be at least four inches below the outlet from the manifold, and the silencer at least 12 inches. In a sailboat, the silencer should be as close to the centerline of the boat as possible. If it is set off to one side, at extreme angles of heel on one tack it may end up close to the level of the manifold and water could surge back into the engine.

In most boats, especially sailboats, the silencer ends up well below the boat's waterline. If water were to flow into the exhaust pipe, or to flow steadily through the water-injection pipe in the exhaust manifold, the silencer could set up a siphoning action that would fill it and then fill the exhaust pipe into the exhaust manifold. If any of the exhaust valves were open when the engine shut down, this water would flow into the engine. Expensive damage would almost certainly result. Therefore, water lift type exhausts must be installed with the following three safeguards (see Figure 14-6):

1. The raw-water injection line must be carried well above sea level (to the underside of the deck) and fitted with an anti-siphon valve. These simple devices, available from Wilcox-Crittenden and others, admit air into the system in such a way as to prevent any siphoning action developing from the raw water inlet side. In salt water, though, they are prone to leaking, and salt water will spray out into the engine room when the engine is running. It is advisable to fit a hose to the top of the valve and to vent it into the cockpit or some other suitable area so that

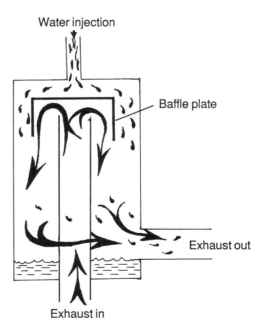

Figure 14-5. *A modified wet silencer.*

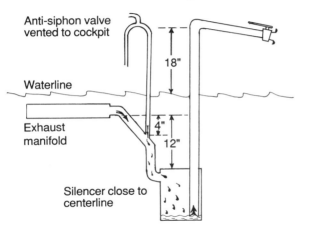

Anti-siphon valve
vented to cockpit

18"

Waterline

Exhaust
manifold

4"

12"

Silencer close to
centerline

Figure 14-6. *Arrangement of water lift-type
exhaust and silencer.*

any spray is taken harmlessly out of the engine room.

2. The exhaust hose itself should be looped as high as possible above the water line to stop following seas from driving up it. Carried too far, however, this will create a harmful rise in exhaust back pressure, especially on turbocharged engines.

3. The exhaust should have a readily accessible cutoff valve, which can be closed when the engine is shut down at sea.

The North Sea exhaust design illustrated in Figure 14-4 uses a slightly different wet exhaust. In this instance, the silencer is set above the engine; the exhaust gases come up a pipe inside it. The water injection sprays in the top of the silencer over a baffle plate (Figure 14-5). The water and gases exit from the bottom of this silencer. Because the exhaust gases do not have to lift the injected water, this system results in less back pressure than the more usual water-lift type. This is better for turbocharged engines. On the other side of the coin, the result of reduced back pressure is more noise.

Engine beds

Many modern boats are lightweight and flexible. An engine, on the other hand, is ex-

tremely rigid—necessarily so. An engine crankcase and block are designed to withstand all the internal stresses and tendency to flex generated by the moving parts. However, if the engine is rigidly bolted down to engine beds that flex, some serious problems can arise.

1. The engine crankcase may be distorted (even if only by a thousandth of an inch or so) imposing severe stresses on the crankshaft, which could lead to eventual crankshaft failure.

2. The engine and propeller shaft alignment may be thrown out, leading to excessive vibration, wear of the bearings in the gearbox, or reduction gear, and wear of the stern tube bearing (generally a cutlass bearing).

Most modern boats have engines mounted on flexible feet, and they have flexible propeller shaft couplings. This is still no substitute for adequate engine beds and proper alignment with the propeller shaft. In a rigid enough hull, it is still hard to beat the smooth running of a properly installed and aligned, rigidly bolted engine and rigid propeller shaft coupling.

Engine beds have to transfer the stresses generated by the engine to the hull of the boat, and at the same time stiffen the hull as much as possible so that hull deflection due to wave action is not transmitted to the engine. The longer the beds, in general, the greater their effect, though clearly they must *in themselves* be strong enough to resist the bending forces applied to them. A thin piece of wood, for example, bonded to the side of the hull will flex along with it and serve no purpose, regardless of length. *On the other hand, improperly installed rigid engine beds in a flexible hull can set up localized stresses which may lead to hull failure.*

The engine bed must incorporate some kind of a drip pan to catch any oil that leaks from the engine. These are Coast Guard regulations—allowing any engine oil to leak into the general sump and be discharged overboard is strictly illegal and carries heavy penalties. This regulation is enforced.

Engine alignment

Correct engine alignment with the propeller shaft is critical to the reduction of vibration and a long life for the gearbox, reduction gear, and stern-tube bearings. Flexible mounts and couplings are no substitute for correct engine alignment—their function is to dampen vibration and to deal with distortion due to the hull flexing, and so on, not to compensate for misalignment. The following procedure is applicable to all engine installations.

Engine alignment can be a tedious business, but patience is the order of the day. The purpose is to bring the coupling on the engine drive shaft into a near-perfect fit with the coupling on the propeller shaft. This is done by taking a series of measurements between the faces of the two couplings, but in order for these to be meaningful, the couplings must have absolutely square faces, be exactly of the same diameter, have their shaft holes exactly in the center, and be installed absolutely squarely on their respective shafts. Some exaggerated drawings should help to make this clear (Figure 14-7).

The couplings and shaft should be taken to a machine shop and *dressed up* in a lathe. New couplings and shafts should always be mated up and machined before installation. The couplings must fit tightly to their shafts because any play at this point will throw out the face of the coupling in relation to its shaft. Once in the boat, this relationship between a coupling and its shaft can only be checked with a dial indicator, a specialized measuring instrument. It may be necessary to hire a mechanic to check what is called face (or flange) runout and bore runout (see Figure 14-8).

Engine alignment should be attempted only with the boat in the water, and with normal ballast, water, fuel, and stores on board, so that the hull takes up its most usual position. The engine is moved into approximate alignment with its propeller shaft, and then fine-tuning begins, jacking the engine first this way, and then that, until a near-exact coincidence is achieved.

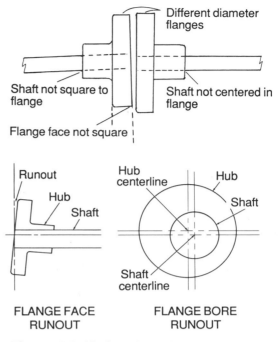

Figure 14-7 *Shaft and coupling problems affecting engine alignment. (Courtesy Caterpillar Tractor Co.)*

Some engines have adjustable feet, which is a tremendous help. Others use thin pieces of metal that you slide under the feet to adjust their height. This is known as shim stock and can be bought in thicknesses from 0.001″ to 0.025″ from reputable automotive stores or engineering supply houses. A variety of thicknesses will be needed.

The bore alignment is the first to be adjusted. A straightedge (such as a steel ruler) is held across the outside of the coupling flanges at the top and bottom, and each side. The engine is moved around until all four sides are parallel (see Figure 14-8).

If the propeller shaft has a long, unsupported section emerging from the stern tube and stuffing box, however, the shaft will droop down and give a false indication of bore alignment. On larger boats one has to calculate half the weight of the protruding shaft, add to it the whole weight of the coupling mounted on it, and then pull up on the

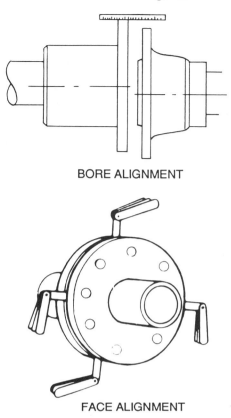

BORE ALIGNMENT

FACE ALIGNMENT

Figure 14-8. *Bore and face alignment. (Courtesy Caterpillar Tractor Co.)*

coupling by this amount with a spring scale (such as is used for weighing fish). On smaller boats, you can move the shaft up and down by hand and get a very good idea of the center point, and then the shaft can be supported with an appropriately sized block of wood with a V cut in it to hold the shaft and allow it to be rotated.

Most couplings have a machined recess on one half, into which a raised face on the other half fits. When bore alignment is correct, the two will slip together with a smooth and easy feel—no amount of forcing is permissible. Even when bore alignment seems correct, the coupling faces may still be misaligned, and this problem has to now be addressed (see Figure 14-8).

The two coupling faces are brought to within a few thousandths of an inch of one another, and feeler gauges are used to measure the gap at top and bottom, and both sides. Only when all four are equal are the two faces correctly aligned. In moving the engine around to straighten out this face alignment, however, the bore alignment frequently gets upset. This must now be rechecked, and then the face alignment once again, and so on until both are just right. At this point the gap between the coupling halves should be measured at the top, and then the coupling rotated and the gap measured at the same point as it moves around. If the gap changes, then there is runout in the shaft or coupling and you must go back to square one and trace the problem. To doublecheck the accuracy of this last test, the coupling should be rotated a full 360° and the gap rechecked at the top once more. If it has changed, it means that the coupling halves moved during the test and the test is invalid. For this test to be meaningful, the gap at the top must be the same at the beginning and end of the 360° rotation of the coupling.

If all measurements are satisfactory, only now is the engine bolted down, making sure that it is resting evenly on all its feet or the crankcase may be distorted. After bolting down, the alignment is checked yet again—half the time tightening up the engine bolts throws it out!

Engine alignments can drive one to drink. It is a process that cannot be short-circuited. As a general rule of thumb, the difference in the gap from one side of a flange to another should not exceed 0.001″ for every inch of flange diameter (i.e., 0.005″—five thousandths of an inch—on a five-inch-diameter coupling). Only when the clearances are *within* this tolerance can the coupling be bolted up.

Engine alignment needs checking periodically—certainly anytime vibration develops in the propeller shaft, though this may be caused by a fouled or bent propeller, a bent propeller shaft or strut, or worn bearings. It should always be rechecked with a new engine after the first 25 hours of running time.

Auxiliary equipment

An increasing amount of extra equipment is driven off the engine these days, including alternators, bilge pumps, hydraulic pumps, refrigeration compressors, and AC generators. The normal method is to fasten a small auxiliary shaft to the forward end of the crankshaft, install a couple of pulleys on it, and drive the equipment via belts from these pulleys. The following are one or two caveats that spring to mind.

1. Equipment mounted in this fashion exerts a sideways pull on the auxiliary shaft. There is a strict limit to how much side loading an engine can tolerate without damaging crankshaft oil seals and bearings. The manufacturer's specifications will have to be checked to see that this is not exceeded.

2. The driving pulleys on the stub shaft must be in correct alignment with the driven pulleys on the auxiliary equipment. A straight steel rod held in the groove of one pulley should drop cleanly into the groove on the other pulley. This should be repeated on both sides of the pulleys. Figure 14-9 gives examples of pulley misalignment.

3. If an engine is mounted on flexible feet but the auxiliary equipment is rigidly mounted to the hull side or a bulkhead, as the engine flexes it will alter the drive-belt tension, which may cause problems. A corollary to this is that certain pieces of equipment (notably reciprocal refrigeration compressors) when mounted to the hull side are capable of flexing the engine on its feet and pulling it out of alignment with its propeller shaft. The solution to such a problem is to mount the equipment on the engine itself.

4. The impact of the additional loads of the auxiliary equipment on engine cranking speeds, and therefore ease of starting, must be taken into consideration.

Vibration analysis

The following is excerpted, with thanks, from Caterpillar's *Marine Engines Application and Installation Guide*, published in October 1982, page 39.

The causes of linear vibrations can usually be identified by determining if:

1. The vibration amplitudes increase with the speed. If so, they are probably caused by centrifugal forces causing bending of components of the drive shafts. Checks should be made for unbalance and misalignment.

2. The vibrations occur within a narrow speed range. This normally occurs on equipment attached to the machinery —pipes, air cleaners, etc. When vibrations show maximum amplitude or *peak out* at a narrow speed range, the vibrating component is in *resonance*. These vibrations can be modified by changing the natural frequency of the part by stiffening or softening its mounting.

3. The vibrations increase as a load is applied. This is caused by torque reaction and can be corrected by mounting the engine or driven equipment more securely or by stiffening the base or foundation. Defective or worn couplings can also cause this problem.

Maintenance

Every engine installation should be designed to maximize ease of access to the key points

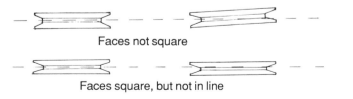

Faces not square

Faces square, but not in line

Figure 14-9. *Pulley misalignment.*

of maintenance, specifically:

1. the oil filter;
2. the air filter;
3. fuel filters;
4. the water and sediment drain, or pump, from the fuel tank;
5. the water pump;
6. all drain points in the cooling and exhaust systems;
7. all grease points;
8. the propeller shaft coupling;
9. the stuffing box on the stern tube.

The first substantial overhaul is likely to be a decoke—you must have room to work on and remove the cylinder head and pistons. In the case of marinized truck engines, which require the removal of the pan (sump) to pull the pistons, some thought will have to be put into how this can be done *when the engine is first installed*, rather than when it ceases to run through loss of compression.

Warning devices and instrumentation

The regular instrumentation generally includes an oil-pressure gauge or warning light, a water-temperature gauge, a charging light, and a tachometer.

An oil-pressure warning light is of little use. By the time it comes on, any problem is likely to have gotten out of hand. A pressure gauge, by contrast, is an essential piece of equipment. Likewise, a charging light gives very little information—an ammeter, which

will show how much charge is actually being fed to the battery, is far more useful, as is a voltmeter to show the state of charge of the batteries.

When an engine is used infrequently, it is hard to keep track of its running hours, and therefore maintenance intervals. An engine-hour clock, which records total running hours, is a very handy instrument to have.

The two critical indicators of a serious engine malfunction are the cooling water temperature and the oil pressure. It is a worthwhile investment to fit alarm gauges to these. If the temperature rises above a certain set point or the oil pressure falls below the set point, the indicating needle on the gauge touches an electrical contact and closes a circuit.

The alarm circuit can be wired to a light and bell, to an automatic shut down device, or both. The latter is normally a solenoid valve on the fuel line or injection pump fuel-control rack—when the solenoid is energized or de-energized (depending on how it is wired) it closes off the fuel supply to the engine.

An automatic shutdown has its drawbacks. It is one more piece of electronic equipment to malfunction. What is more, there may come a life and death situation during which an engine problem triggers the alarm. The captain should have the option to risk the engine in order to attempt to save the boat.

Chapter Fifteen

Engine Selection

Power and torque

Engines are generally compared primarily on the basis of their horsepower (h.p.) ratings, but this is not necessarily the best way to judge either their applicability in a given situation or even the *usable* power produced. This chapter takes up such questions, but first, some definitions:

Indicated horsepower (IHP). IHP is the total power developed *within the engine cylinders* through the burning of the diesel fuel —it is a theoretical figure, with no practical application in our context.

Friction horsepower (FHP). Otherwise known as friction losses, this is the amount of energy consumed *by the engine* in order to work. It consists principally of energy losses caused by friction between moving parts; windage resistance to moving parts, especially large flywheels; pumping losses, the resistance to air and gas flow in the inlet and exhaust systems; and work required to drive the camshaft, valves, and auxiliary equipment (alternator, water pump, etc.).

Brake horsepower (BHP). BHP is the *usable* energy put out by the engine. It is determined by subtracting the friction losses from the indicated horsepower (BHP = IHP − FHP). The BHP is generally 50 to 85% of the IHP and is almost always the figure used to define the horsepower rating of an engine in manufacturers' publicity material. Engines are sometimes rated at their *maximum*

power output, but this is generally not sustainable for more than a few minutes at a time without risking damage to the engine. The rating a boat owner is interested in is the continuous-duty rating, the maximum BHP available on a continuous basis.

Shaft horsepower (SHP). Shaft horsepower is the energy actually transmitted through the engine drive shaft. It can be measured directly at the engine (before any transmission, reverse gearing, reduction gearing, etc., has been fitted), in which case it is more or less synonymous with BHP; after the gearing, in which case it will be reduced from engine SHP by the resistance generated by friction in the gearing; or at the propeller, in which case it will accurately reflect the actual power being transmitted to the propeller—what I like to think of as *usable* energy.

All gearing absorbs power. A high-speed, lightweight diesel may require a higher reduction gear ratio than a slower-revving engine. In certain instances, while a high-speed engine may have a greater BHP rating than a slower one, the latter may actually produce more usable energy at the propeller shaft. Whenever the power output of engines is compared, the most useful figure is the SHP rating *at the propeller shaft*.

Torque. Torque is a twisting force, creating rotation. It is measured in foot pounds. If a foot-long lever were attached to the end of a shaft, a spring gauge like those used to weigh fish were hooked up to the end of the lever, and a rotating force were then applied to the shaft, the gauge would register a reading in pounds. The greater the rotating force, the higher the reading, and the number of pounds of force applied to the shaft, when measured at the end of the one-foot lever arm, would represent torque.

Engine manufacturers frequently give a torque rating for their engines. Once again, one must determine whether this is a rating before or after reduction and reverse gearing. Torque ratings *at the propeller* are a very valuable way of comparing engines and of determining what size propeller each can swing. It is quite possible for two engines with very different BHP ratings to have the same, or nearly the same, torque rating at the propeller (depending on gearing and other factors). To determine the total power available from the torque rating, one must multiply it by the engine speed. Each of two engines may generate 100 foot-pounds of torque at the propeller, but one may be able to sustain it at twice the speed of the other, and so generate twice the maximum thrust:

Power = Torque × Speed (r.p.m.).

When you select an engine, you must distinguish between boats with displacement hulls and those with planing hulls. A displacement hull is one that remains constantly immersed at all times, whereas a planing hull develops hydrodynamic forces at high speed that move it up onto the surface of the water.

A displacement hull has a predetermined top speed (defined as hull speed) more or less irrespective of available power. This top speed is governed by wave theory, and is approximately $1.34 \times \sqrt{\text{LWL}}$ (1.34 times the square root of the boat's waterline length). A planing hull, on the other hand, breaks free of the constraints imposed by wave theory, and its top speed is more closely related to available power.

Wave theory

As a boat moves through water it makes waves, which behave according to certain physical laws—the faster the waves move, the wider apart they are spaced. The distance from one wave crest to the next is the *wave length*. As a boat picks up speed, so too does its associated wave formation, and the faster it goes, the farther apart the waves become. It is possible to construct a table showing the speed of waves of any particular length, or conversely, the length of waves of any particular speed (Figure 15-1).

A boat eventually reaches a speed at which the length of its associated wave formation is the same as its waterline length— one wave crest is at the bow (the bow wave), and the next is at the stern (the stern wave). If the boat were to go any faster, its wave formation would also speed up and therefore lengthen; the boat would move ahead of its stern wave, its stern would sink into the trough between the bow and stern waves, and its bow would appear to be climbing the bow wave. In a sense, the boat would be dragging its stern wave, requiring tremendous amounts of power. As a consequence, the maximum speed of a displacement hull (its hull speed) is determined by the speed of the wave formation with a wavelength equal to the waterline length of the boat. The longer a boat's waterline length, the farther apart its bow and stern waves will be and

VELOCITY IN KNOTS	WAVE LENGTH IN FEET
1	0.56
2	2.23
3	5.01
4	8.90
5	13.90
6	20.0
7	27.2
8	35.6
9	45.0
10	55.6
11	67.3
12	80.1
13	94.0
14	109.0
15	125.2

Figure 15-1. *Table of periods and lengths of sea waves.*

therefore the faster the boat can go. This is why a sailboat with long overhangs can move faster when it is heeled than when it is upright—the heeling increases the waterline length.

Figure 15-1 shows how dramatically wavelengths increase with small increases in speed. To double a displacement boat's hull speed from 5 to 10 knots requires a fourfold increase in the waterline length.

The illustrations in Figure 15-2 show different wave formations associated with a 32-foot-waterline boat moving at different speeds. Only in the most exceptional circumstances, such as when a boat surfs down the face of a wave, can a displacement hull exceed its hull speed. The more closely hull speed is approached, the greater the increase in power required for a given increase in speed. A 32-foot boat can be driven fairly close to its hull speed in smooth water by considerably less than 20 h.p. At around

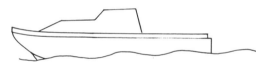

A 32-foot (waterline length) boat moving at 4 knots. There will be approximately 3½ waves to its length.

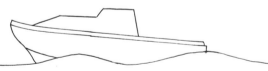

The same boat moving at 7½ knots. There will be approximately one wave to its length. This boat is moving at hull speed for displacement boats of that length.

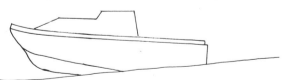

The boat is now moving at, say, 12 knots. It has moved up onto the surface of the water and ahead of its own wave formation.

Figure 15-2. *Boat speed and wave formations.*

75% of hull speed, the boat is extremely efficient, but beyond this point, the additional fuel burned becomes increasingly disproportionate to the increase in speed, due to the rapid rise in drag.

A planing hull, on the other hand, breaks free of its own wave formation by moving up onto the surface of the water. The point at which this occurs can frequently be felt as a sudden surge in speed. In the bottom of Figure 15-2 a planing hull is shown ahead of its own wave formation, the point at which powerboats with flat sterns really begin to accelerate, barely skimming the surface of the water.

Power requirements of displacement hulls

The graph shown in Figure 15-3 gives some idea of the approximate horsepower required to drive a displacement boat at hull speed.

The graph is entered on the bottom line at the appropriate LWL (waterline length) and traced upward until the curve is intersected. Moving horizontally across the graph to the left-hand margin, you can read the required power. It is normal to make an additional allowance of around 33% for adverse conditions, and if the engine is to be coupled to a power take-off shaft and used to drive auxiliary equipment—such as a belt-driven generator, refrigeration unit, or

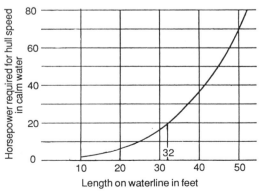

Figure 15-3. *Determining required horsepower.*

saltwater wash-down pump—more power will be needed. This graph merely seeks to give a fair average.

A more accurate method for determining required horsepower is given in Francis S. Kinney's *Skene's Elements of Yacht Design.* Starting from the boat's waterline length—let us assume 32 feet—Kinney uses a speed/length ratio of 1.30 × √LWL (which equals 7.35 knots for a waterline length of 32 feet) as a basis for determining engine power. The graph shown in Figure 15-4 is entered on the bottom line at 1.30 and traced upward to the lower curve for light-displacement hulls and to the upper curve for heavy-displacement. Let us assume a heavy cruising boat of 26,000 pounds. Using the upper curve, we move horizontally to find the resistance in pounds for each long ton of displacement (a long ton = 2,240 lbs.). For a speed/length ratio of 1.30, the resistance is 45 lbs. per long ton (26,000 lbs = 11.6 long tons). Therefore, total resistance at hull speed (7.35 knots) for this hull is:

$$11.6 \times 45 = 522 \text{ lbs.}$$

Effective horsepower (EHP) is given by the formula:

$$\begin{aligned} \text{EHP} &= \text{Resistance} \times \text{Speed} \times 0.003 \\ &= 522 \times 7.35 \times 0.003 \\ &= 11.50 \text{ h.p.} \end{aligned}$$

Propellers are notoriously inefficient at

transmitting power. Kinney uses the following factors:

> Folding two-blade: 10%
> Auxiliary two-blade: 35–45%
> Three-blade: 50%

Let us assume an efficient auxiliary two-bladed propeller with a 45% rating. We arrive at the following horsepower to drive our boat at hull speed:

$$11.50/0.45 = 25.5 \text{ h.p.}$$

Kinney also adds 33% for adverse conditions to give a maximum power requirement in this example of 34 h.p. Note that this calculation has been made on the basis of very close to hull speed (1.30 × √LWL). If the same calculation is made on the basis of approximately 75% of hull speed (1.00 × √LWL = 5.7 knots) the horsepower requirement is only 8.5. This dramatically illustrates the increase in drag, and therefore fuel consumption, as hull speed is approached.

Selecting an engine size

Almost all sailboats have displacement hulls. For every boat that is underpowered and overloaded, there is one that is overpowered. This adds unnecessary weight and expense, takes up unnecessary space, and can even be harmful to the engine because diesels like to run at or near full load. (Because of the difficulty of precisely metering the minute amounts of fuel at light loads, diesels tend to idle unevenly, resulting in poor combustion and excessive carbon formation.)

In sailboats up to 40 feet in overall length, 10 to 20 h.p. is perfectly adequate for maneuvering in and out of moorings, setting anchors, charging batteries, and running auxiliary equipment. For the loss of a knot or so of maximum speed, there are major gains in terms of lower cost, lighter weight, smaller size, and cheaper overhauls. The boat, however, might be underpowered in strong headwinds, rough seas, adverse currents, or with a foul, heavily barnacled bottom.

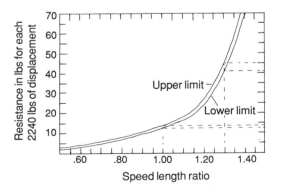

Figure 15-4. *Curves covering range of resistance for displacement-type hulls. (Courtesy Dodd Mead and Co.)*

Planing hulls, on the other hand, are a different matter altogether. A planing hull really only becomes efficient when it is free of its own wave formation and on top of the water, and it takes a considerable amount of energy to achieve this. An underpowered planing hull may never get up and go, in which case it will remain forever locked into the same constraints as a displacement hull.

Two extremes

At this point it might be interesting to consider two extreme examples: a heavy displacement cruising sailboat and a lightweight sportfishing boat.

A heavy-displacement cruising sailboat

Engine size can be determined using Kinney's formulas. Weight is not of too much concern. The owner is principally interested in reliability, simplicity, longevity, and ease of maintenance. This suggests a relatively slow-turning, naturally aspirated, raw-water-cooled, traditional marine diesel. The slow speed promotes a long life; natural aspiration does away with all the complications of a turbocharger and intercooler, and this in turn enables raw-water cooling to be used instead of a heat exchanger. Every part of the engine will be easily accessible, and even cylinder head removal will not involve too much work.

This owner might add a few more requirements. Since his plans involve long-range cruising, the engine should have hand-start capability in case the battery goes dead in some remote anchorage. For similar reasons, a cold-start device based on adding oil to the cylinders is preferred over one (such as glow plugs) requiring battery power.

This particular owner expects to encounter extremely severe weather and therefore wants no hatches in the cockpit that might leak. In effect, once the engine is installed in the boat, the cockpit will be built over it—the only way to get the engine out again will be in pieces. Therefore, it must be possible to rebuild the engine *completely* in situ. Such a requirement calls for an engine

that allows access to the connecting rod caps and that permits the crankshaft to be removed without having to move the engine off its bed or drop the pan (sump). The engine will need wet cylinder liners, and preferably replaceable valve seats and guides in the cylinder head.

This extreme is perhaps best represented by the Sabb range of marine diesel engines. They have huge flywheels, massive weight, and tremendous reputation for reliability in the treacherous conditions of the North Sea.

A lightweight sportfishing boat

The maximum power for the minimum weight is critical to this environment. Tests on sportfishing boats have shown that outboard motors with less power will give higher top speeds and greater fuel economy than more powerful inboard gasoline engines. (See, for example, *Boating* magazine, February 1986, page 102, "Outboard v. Inboard." I am not aware of any similar tests with diesel engines.) The critical factors at work here are the extra weight of the inboard engine(s), and its placement farther forward than the transom-mounted outboards.

This gives some idea of the supreme importance of maximizing the power-to-weight ratio in this kind of craft. This also indicates the use of relatively high-revving diesels. All other things being equal, if one engine the same size as another is run twice as fast, it

Figure 15-5. *A traditional marine diesel—Sabb 2JZ. (Courtesy Sabb Motor A.S.)*

can suck in twice as much air and develop twice as much power. In order to further boost power, a turbocharger and intercooler will be needed, and the engine will have to be run at higher operating temperatures. This will necessitate a freshwater cooling system and heat exchanger.

The owner of this boat expects to dock in a marina every night. He has no need for hand-starting, decompression levers, or oil-based cold-starting devices—the far more convenient glow plugs will be used. The more complicated maintenance procedures are likewise not of concern. Maintenance will be carried out by the marina's mechanic, and the engine(s), housed under a console on the main deck, can be removed from the boat fairly easily for major overhauls.

There are numerous high-speed, light-weight, turbocharged and intercooled diesels on the market today suitable for this application.

The power train

The power train is a general expression to describe gearbox, reduction gear, and propeller arrangements. Just as there are no right and wrong choices when it comes to engines—merely ones that are more appropriate for specific situations—so too with the power train.

Figure 15-6. *A turbocharged diesel—Caterpillar 3208. (Courtesy Caterpillar Tractor Co.)*

Some mention has already been made of the power losses created by reverse and reduction gearing. You might wonder why manufacturers do not use a direct drive and dispense with the power losses of a reduction gear. This is indeed done on large ships where the engines turn over at speeds as low as 300 r.p.m. In fact, many of these engines have two camshafts and two sets of valves so that they can be stopped and restarted backward for reverse, thus eliminating the need for a reverse gear. High-speed diesel engines in lightweight high-speed boats also frequently have a direct drive to the propeller, though a reverse gear is required. But on slower, heavier boats, especially displacement hulls, the high propeller speeds of direct drive would create excessive propeller slip and cavitation.

Slip

A propeller is specified according to its diameter, its pitch, and whether it is left- or right-handed. The latter merely indicates which way the propeller turns to produce forward motion; the diameter is self-evident. Pitch is a little more complex.

The blades of a propeller are set at an angle to its hub (boss or center). As the propeller turns, the angled faces cut into the water, and in the process, pressure is created on the rear side of the blade while a vacuum is formed on the front edge (just as with the upper edge of an airplane wing). The two together impart motion to the boat.

In a perfect environment, no motion would be imparted to the water, and the propeller would move ahead by the total amount of the deflection of its blades. In practice, of course, some movement forward of the propeller (and therefore the boat) takes place, while at the same time water is driven back past the propeller. In the perfect environment, the greater the angle of deflection of the propeller blade (within reason) the farther the propeller would move in one revolution. This theoretical distance, measured in inches, is the propeller *pitch*. A 12-pitch propeller would move forward 12", a 16-pitch propeller, 16". In real life, the 12-pitch propeller might move the boat forward 6″ per revolution, the difference between this figure and the theoretical movement representing the degree of *slip*—in this case 50%.

The degree of slip will obviously vary with circumstances, but is generally 20 to 50%. On intitial start-up, when the boat is dead in the water and there is a lot of inertia to overcome, a considerable push will be needed to get it moving, and this will show up as a high degree of slip. Once the boat gains momentum, slip will lessen. Punching into a head sea, slip will be much higher than in smooth water, approaching 100% in extreme conditions.

Cavitation

Cavitation occurs when a propeller loses contact with the water in which it is turning and sucks air down from the atmospheric interface. This phenomenon is normally the result of a propeller turning too fast *in a specific situation*. If the diesel engines on most displacement boats were directly coupled to their propellers, cavitation would result. As a consequence it is almost always necessary to gear down the engine with a reduction gear; 2 to 1 (2:1) and 3 to 1 (3:1) are the most common ratios, but on occasion reduction gears as high as 5:1 or even 7:1 are used.

Propeller selection

As shaft speeds are reduced, propeller diameter or pitch must be increased to maintain thrust. The optimum combination of propeller diameter, pitch, and speed can only be determined individually, because two identical boats may have different requirements. For example, one sailboat may be used for racing, while another is used for cruising in areas with light and variable winds. The former owner wants a propeller that gives the least resistance when not in use and will probably choose a folding two-blade, accepting the inevitable inefficiencies under power. The latter owner expects to do quite a bit of motorsailing and will be looking for efficiency under power—a fairly sizable three-blade propeller will probably be chosen, despite the increased drag under sail.

In general, large slow-turning propellers suffer less from slip and cavitation than do small high-revving propellers, but the larger propellers create far more drag when idle. Three-bladed propellers are more efficient than two-bladed ones, but again the three blades create more drag and can slow a boat under sail by up to a full knot. Two-bladed propellers, especially on boats with an enclosed propeller aperture and deadwood, sometimes create some vibration as the two blades pass through the relatively still water behind the deadwood. When not in use, however, the two blades can be lined up with the deadwood for less drag.

Unlike an automobile, which has a gearbox to match the engine to differing loads, a boat's propeller is fixed. The engine and power train will only operate at the optimum relationship in one particular set of circumstances. The set of circumstances chosen will relate to boat use. A sportfishing boat, for example, is generally set up for maximum speed in smooth water; a cruising sailboat might well be sized up for maximum efficiency at a little below hull speed, once again in smooth water. At speeds or in conditions different from these, the engine may be overloaded and the propeller may slip or even cavitate.

Whatever the propeller and reduction gear combination chosen, it must be designed to allow the engine to operate *at its full rated speed under full load* (in adverse conditions, and taking into account all auxiliary equipment), and not just in ideal circumstances. Otherwise, engine overloading is an ever-present possibility.

Variable-pitch propellers

The use of a variable-pitch propeller (otherwise known as a *controllable pitch propeller*) eliminates some of these problems. The propeller blades rotate on a central hub (see Figure 15-7), and this rotation of the blades alters the blade pitch and also the direction of thrust—reverse is achieved by turning the blades on the hub, while the propeller itself continues to turn in the same direction. A variable-pitch propeller functions much like the gearbox of an automobile. The blade pitch can be reduced to almost nothing, resembling a low gear on a car, or increased to a very high setting, resembling a high gear.

Just as a heavily laden car uses a low gear to crawl up a steep hill, so a heavy cruising boat punching into a head sea needs a propeller with reduced pitch in order to cut down on slip. The same boat in smooth water is in the position of a car coasting downhill—the highest gear possible will be the most efficient, which translates into more propeller pitch. A variable-pitch propeller makes it possible to match engine output to any conditions for the most efficient thrust.

A prospective boat owner should not necessarily accept the stock power option available off the shelf for the boat under consideration. An analysis of the kind of use anticipated will indicate the amount of overall power required and the optimum propeller combination in terms of diameter, pitch, and maximum propeller speed. Given the choice of a specific engine and propeller, it is then a simple matter to determine the reduction gearing (if any) necessary to mate the two. For example, if it has been determined that a given propeller is desired with a maximum speed of 1,000 r.p.m. and maximum thrust at this speed equivalent to 35 SHP, and an engine has been selected with an output of 40 BHP at 3,500 r.p.m., then 3.5:1 reduction gear will be needed to match the two.

Miscellaneous

Ease of maintenance

It is increasingly common for engine manufacturers to make all the key maintenance points accessible from the front of the engine, something that is especially helpful in many sailboat installations. On all marine engines it should be possible to change the engine oil by pumping it out, instead of having to drop a plug in the pan (sump) and drain it from below.

Availability of spares

Availability of spares is obviously related to the boat's intended cruising waters. If worldwide voyaging is anticipated, you will want to know whether spares are available on a worldwide basis.

What is, and is not, included in the engine price

On some engines, the base price includes a wide range of accessories, but on others, very few at all. The only effective way to compare costs is on the basis of the *total installed cost*—unbudgeted extras may increase the price of an installation by as much as $1,000. These "extras" can include such essential items as the alternator, engine-mounting feet, shaft coupling, instrument panel and wiring harness, exhaust system, heat exchanger, and raw-water cooling pump!

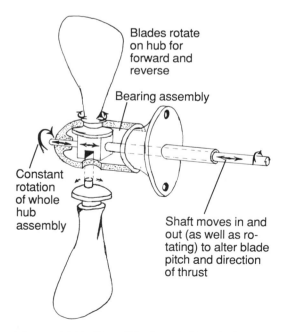

Figure 15-7. *Simplified variable pitch propeller (Sabb type).*

Blades rotate on hub for forward and reverse

Bearing assembly

Constant rotation of whole hub assembly

Shaft moves in and out (as well as rotating) to alter blade pitch and direction of thrust

Some questions to ask about an engine

1. What is its SHP rating (or torque at the propeller) in continuous duty?

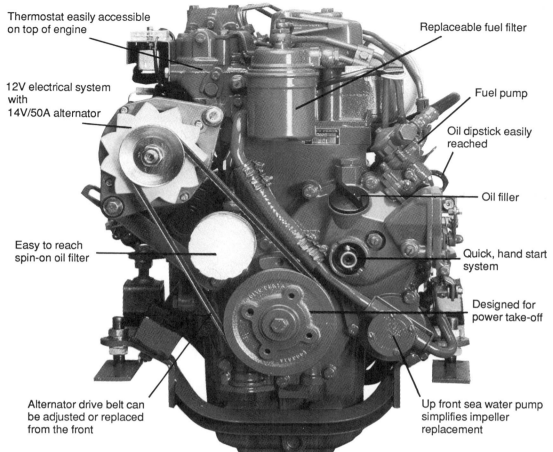

Thermostat easily accessible on top of engine

Replaceable fuel filter

12V electrical system with 14V/50A alternator

Fuel pump

Oil dipstick easily reached

Easy to reach spin-on oil filter

Oil filler

Quick, hand start system

Designed for power take-off

Alternator drive belt can be adjusted or replaced from the front

Up front sea water pump simplifies impeller replacement

Figure 15-8. *Accessible service points—Volvo Penta Series 2000. (Courtesy Volvo Penta.)*

2. What is its maximum r.p.m. in continuous duty?

3. What is the recommended reduction gearing and propeller size (diameter and pitch)? Will this provide the optimum thrust in the conditions anticipated for this boat?

4. Is there a variable-pitch propeller available for this unit?

5. Can the engine be hand-started?

6. Can the engine be rebuilt in situ?

7. Does the engine have replaceable cylinder liners (wet liners), valve guides, and valve seats?

8. Can an auxiliary shaft be fitted? What load will it carry?

9. Is the engine turbocharged, intercooled, raw-water-cooled, or heat-exchanger cooled?

10. What is the engine's fuel consumption at full continuous load?

11. How much does it weigh? What is its power-to-weight ratio (including all necessary auxiliary equipment, such as heat exchangers and header tanks)?

12. How much does it cost and what does this price include?

13. What is the availability of spare parts and service in the boat's anticipated cruising waters?

Appendix A

Tools

A basic set of mechanics tools is required for working on engines—wrenches, a socket set (preferably ½" drive), screwdrivers, hacksaw, crescent wrench, Vise Grips, etc. The tool kit should also include a copy of the appropriate manufacturer's shop manual. This appendix covers one or two more specialized items.

1. **Oil squirt can.** Preferably with a flexible tip, for putting oil into the air inlet manifold.

2. **Grease gun.** Again preferably with a flexible hose.

3. **Feeler (thickness) gauges.** From 0.001" to 0.025" (or the metric equivalent if one's clearances are specified in millimeters).

4. **Oil filter clamp** for spin-on-type filters. Such filters are extremely difficult to get on and off without this special purpose tool. More than one size may be required if the fuel filters are a different size.

5. **Grinding paste.** This is sold in three grades: coarse, medium, and fine. There is very little call for coarse, and the medium and fine can very often be bought in one container.

6. **Suction cup** and **handle** for lapping in valves.

7. **Torque wrench.** An indispensable tool for any serious mechanical work, and probably the most expensive special item, although there are some perfectly serviceable and relatively inexpensive ones on the mar-

ket for occasional use. The wrench will fit ½" drive sockets or other sizes with suitable adaptors.

8. **Ball peen hammer.** Most people have carpenters hammers with a jaw for pulling nails, but in mechanical work, a ball peen hammer is far more useful. Hammers are specified by the weight of the head—an 8-oz. hammer is a good all-around size.

9. **Needlenose pliers.** Handy for all kinds of tasks—side-cutting needlenose pliers also have a wire-cutting jaw, and are preferred.

10. **Scrapers.** For cleaning up old gaskets.

11. **Mallet** or **soft-faced hammer.** A surprisingly valuable tool, especially if one has to knock an aluminum or cast-iron casting that might be cracked by a steel hammer.

12. **Aligning punches.** Invaluable from time to time, especially the long ones (8" to 10"). These punches are tapered—a light one (with a tip around ⅛") and a heavier one (around ¼") will do nicely.

13. **Injector bar.** An injector bar is about 15" long, tapered to a point at one end, and with a heel on the other end. It is a very useful tool for prying or levering.

14. **Allen wrenches.** Almost certainly required at some point. Keep an assortment on hand.

15. **Hydrometer.** Needed for testing batteries. It is best to get one of the inexpensive plastic ones, since the regular glass ones, though more accurate, break sooner or later.

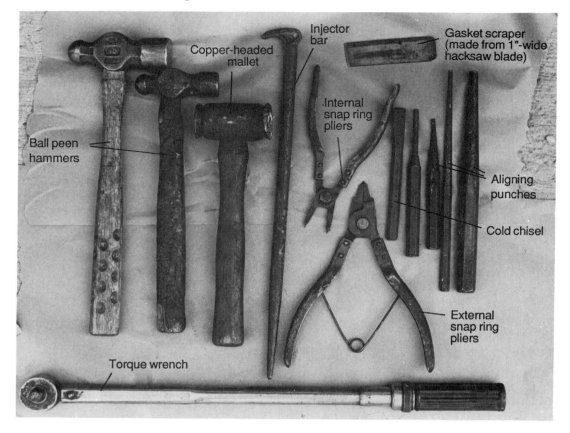

Figure A-1. *Useful tools.*

16. **Snap-ring pliers.** We are now getting into the realm of very specialized equipment for the serious mechanic. Snap rings can almost always be gotten out with needlenose pliers, regular pliers, or the judicious use of screwdrivers.

17. **Valve-spring clamp.**

18. **Piston-ring expander.** This can be dispensed with as indicated in the text.

19. **Piston-ring clamp.**

20. **Gear puller.** These come in all shapes and sizes. There are a number of gears and pulleys in any engine that just cannot be removed, unless you use some kind of a puller, without risking damage to engine castings or other parts. It is frequently possible to improvise, as indicated in the text. What should never be done is to put levers behind a gear to try and force it off—the effort generally ends in failure, and frequently in damage to some casting, the gear, the pulley, or the shaft.

21. **Injector nozzle cleaning set.** Includes a brass-bristle brush and the appropriate nozzle hole prickers for one's injectors. Might be a worthwhile investment for the long-distance cruiser. CAV and others sell these sets with appropriate tools for their own injectors.

A good tool kit represents a considerable expense but will last a lifetime if cared for. In general, *it is not worth buying cheap tools:* sooner or later they break, but long before this point they drive you crazy by slipping and bending. There are quite enough problems in engine work without creating any unnecessary ones.

Appendix B

Spares

The extent of your spare parts inventory will obviously depend on your cruising plans. The following is a fairly comprehensive list with an ocean cruising sailboat in mind. If your plans are less ambitious it can be scaled down appropriately.

1. Oil filters.
2. Fuel filters—quite a number in case a dirty batch of fuel is taken on board and repeated filter changes are needed.
3. An air filter—one only. This should rarely need changing in the marine environment.
4. A raw-water pump overhaul kit, or at the very least, a diaphragm or impeller (depending on the type of pump).
5. A lift-pump overhaul kit, or at the very least, a diaphragm.
6. A fuel injection pump diaphragm if one is fitted.
7. A complete set of belts (alternator, plus auxiliary equipment).
8. An alternator.
9. A starter motor solenoid and Bendix unit.
10. A cylinder head overhaul gasket set.
11. An inlet and exhaust valve.
12. Two sets of valve springs and keepers (exhaust and inlet, if they differ).
13. A set of piston rings.
14. A set of connecting rod bearing shells.
15. One or two injectors, or at the very least matched sets of replacement needle valves and seats and nozzles.
16. A complete set of high-pressure injection lines (from the fuel injection pump to the injectors).
17. A complete engine gasket set.
18. A gearbox oil seal.
19. An O ring kit with an assortment of O rings may one day be worth its weight in gold.
20. A roll of high-temperature gasket paper.
21. A roll of cork-type gasket paper.
22. A tube of gasket compound.
23. Packing for the stern tube stuffing box (Teflon or flax, but not graphite, since this can cause electrolysis).
24. Assorted hose clamps.
25. Flexible fuel line.
26. Hoses.
27. Oil and grease.
28. Penetrating oil.

Appendix C

Useful Tables

This is a rather mixed bag of information that may come in handy at some time or another.

1 HP = 33,000 foot-pounds per minute (550 foot-pounds per second).

$$\text{Torque (in foot-pounds)} = \frac{\text{BHP} \times 5,250}{\text{r.p.m.}}$$

$$\text{BHP} = \frac{\text{Torque} \times \text{r.p.m.}}{5,250}$$

1 Btu = 778 foot-pounds.

1 HP = 2,544 Btus.

1 KW = 1.34 h.p.

1 KW = 3,413 Btus.

100 cubic inches = 1.64 liters.

1 gallon (U.S.) of pure water weighs 8.34 lbs.

1 cubic foot of pure water weighs 62.4 lbs.

1 imperial gallon (U.K.) = 1.2 gallons (U.S.).

Circumference of a circle = $2 \pi R$ or πD, where $\pi = 3.14$.

Area of a circle = πR^2.

Volume of a cylinder = $\pi R^2 \times \text{length}$.

$$°C = \frac{(°F - 32) \times 5}{9}$$

$$°F = \frac{(°C \times 9)}{5} - 32$$

1 short ton (U.S.) = 2,000 lbs.

1 long ton (U.K.) = 2,240 lbs.

Inches	Millimeters	Inches	Millimeters	Inches	Millimeters
0.001	0.0254	0.010	0.2540	0.019	0.4826
0.002	0.0508	0.011	0.2794	0.020	0.5080
0.003	0.0762	0.012	0.3048	0.021	0.5334
0.004	0.1016	0.013	0.3302	0.022	0.5588
0.005	0.1270	0.014	0.3556	0.023	0.5842
0.006	0.1524	0.015	0.3810	0.024	0.6096
0.007	0.1778	0.016	0.4064	0.025	0.6350
0.008	0.2032	0.017	0.4318		
0.009	0.2286	0.018	0.4572		

Figure C-1. *Inches to millimeters conversion table.*

Torque Conversion, Pound Feet/Newton Metres

Pound-Feet (lb.-ft.)	Newton Metres (Nm)	Newton Metres (Nm)	Pound-Feet (lb.-ft.)
1	1.356	1	0.7376
2	2.7	2	1.5
3	4.0	3	2.2
4	5.4	4	3.0
5	6.8	5	3.7
6	8.1	6	4.4
7	9.5	7	5.2
8	10.8	8	5.9
9	12.2	9	6.6
10	13.6	10	7.4
15	20.3	15	11.1
20	27.1	20	14.8
25	33.9	25	18.4
30	40.7	30	22.1
35	47.5	35	25.8
40	54.2	40	29.5
45	61.0	50	36.9
50	67.8	60	44.3
55	74.6	70	51.6
60	81.4	80	59.0
65	88.1	90	66.4
70	94.9	100	73.8
75	101.7	110	81.1
80	108.5	120	88.5
90	122.0	130	95.9
100	135.6	140	103.3
110	149.1	150	110.6
120	162.7	160	118.0
130	176.3	170	125.4
140	189.8	180	132.8
150	203.4	190	140.1
160	216.9	200	147.5
170	230.5	225	166.0
180	244.0	250	184.4

Figure C-2. *Metric conversion table.*

Fraction, decimal, and metric equivalents

Fractions	Decimal In.	Metric mm.	Fractions	Decimal In.	Metric mm.
1/64	.015625	.397	33/64	.515625	13.097
1/32	.03125	.794	17/32	.53125	13.494
3/64	.046875	1.191	35/64	.546875	13.891
1/16	.0625	1.588	9/16	.5625	14.288
5/64	.078125	1.984	37/64	.578125	14.684
3/32	.09375	2.381	19/32	.59375	15.081
7/64	.109375	2.778	39/64	.609375	15.478
1/8	.125	3.175	5/8	.625	15.875
9/64	.140625	3.572	41/64	.640625	16.272
5/32	.15625	3.969	21/32	.65625	16.669
11/64	.171875	4.366	43/64	.671875	17.066
3/16	.1875	4.763	11/16	.6875	17.463
13/64	.203125	5.159	45/64	.703125	17.859
7/32	.21875	5.556	23/32	.71875	18.256
15/64	.234375	5.953	47/64	.734375	18.653
1/4	.250	6.35	3/4	.750	19.05
17/64	.265625	6.747	49/64	.765625	19.447
9/32	.28125	7.144	25/32	.78125	19.844
19/64	.296875	7.54	51/64	.796875	20.241
5/16	.3125	7.938	13/16	.8125	20.638
21/64	.328125	8.334	53/64	.828125	21.034
11/32	.34375	8.731	27/32	.84375	21.431
23/64	.359375	9.128	55/64	.859375	21.828
3/8	.375	9.525	7/8	.875	22.225
25/64	.390625	9.922	57/64	.890625	22.622
13/32	.40625	10.319	29/32	.90625	23.019
27/64	.421875	10.716	59/64	.921875	23.416
7/16	.4375	11.113	15/16	.9375	23.813
29/64	.453125	11.509	61/64	.953125	24.209
15/32	.46875	11.906	31/32	.96875	24.606
31/64	.484375	12.303	63/64	.984375	25.003
1/2	.500	12.7	1	1.00	25.4

Glossary

Aftercooler. Also called an intercooler. A heat exchanger fitted between a turbocharger and an engine air-inlet manifold in order to cool the incoming air.

Alignment. The bringing together of two coupling halves in near-perfect horizontal and vertical agreement.

Ambient. The surrounding temperature, pressure, or both.

Annealing. A process of softening metals.

Atmospheric pressure. The pressure of air at the surface of the earth, conventionally taken to be 14.7 psi.

Atomization. The process of breaking up diesel fuel into minute particles as it is sprayed into an engine cylinder.

Babbitt. A soft white metal alloy frequently used to line replaceable shell-type engine bearings.

Back pressure. A build-up of pressure in an exhaust system.

BHP (Brake Horsepower). The actual power output of an engine at the flywheel.

Bleeding. The process of purging air from a fuel system.

Blow-by. The escape of gases past piston rings or closed valves.

Bottom Dead Center (BDC). A term used to describe the position of a crankshaft when the #1 piston is at the very bottom of its stroke.

Btu (British thermal unit). The unit used to measure quantities of heat.

Butterfly valve. A hinged flap connected to a throttle that is used to close off the air inlet manifold on gasoline engines and some diesel engines.

Cams. Elliptical protrusions on a camshaft.

Camshaft. A shaft with cams, used to operate the valve mechanism on an engine.

Cavitation. The process by which a propeller sucks down air and loses contact with the water in which it is turning.

Circlips. See snap rings.

Collets. See keepers.

Combustion chamber. The space left in a cylinder (and cylinder head) when a piston is at the top of its stroke.

Common rail. A type of fuel injection system in which fuel circulates to all the injectors all of the time. Each injector contains its own injection pump with this system.

Compression ratio. The volume of a compression chamber with the piston at the top of its stroke as a proportion of the total volume of the cylinder when the piston is at the bottom of its stroke.

Connecting rod. The rod connecting a piston to a crankshaft.

Connecting rod bearing. The bearing at the crankshaft end of a connecting rod.

Connecting rod cap. The housing that bolts to the end of a connecting rod, holding it to a crankshaft.

Crank. An offset section of a crankshaft to which a connecting rod is attached.

Cranking speed. The speed at which a starter motor turns over an engine.

Crankshaft. The main rotating member in the base of an engine, transmitting power to the flywheel and power train.

Cutlass bearing. A rubber-sleeved bearing in the stern of a boat that supports the propeller shaft.

Cylinder block. The housing on an engine that contains the cylinders.

Cylinder head. A casting containing the valves and injector that bolts to the top of a cylinder block and seals off the cylinders.

Cylinder liner. A machined sleeve that is pressed into a cylinder block and in which a piston moves up and down.

Decarbonizing. The process of removing carbon from the inside surfaces of an engine and of refurbishing the valves and pistons.

Decompression levers. Levers that hold the exhaust valves open so that no compression pressure is built up, making it easy to turn the engine over.

Dial indicator. A sensitive measuring instrument used in alignment work.

Displacement. The total swept volume of an engine's cylinders expressed in cubic inches or liters.

Distributor pump. A type of fuel injection pump using one central pumping element with a rotating distributor head that sends the fuel to each cylinder in turn.

Dribble. Drops of unatomized fuel entering a cylinder through faulty injection.

Feeler (thickness) gauges. Thin strips of metal machined to precise thicknesses and used for measuring small gaps.

Flyweight. A small pivoted weight used in mechanical governors.

Friction Horsepower. The proportion of the power generated by an engine consumed in the operation of the engine itself (from friction, and from driving water and injection pumps, camshafts, etc.).

Fuel injection pump. A device for metering precise quantities of fuel at precise times and raising them up to injection pressures.

Garboard. The side plank closest to the keel on a wooden boat.

Gasket. A piece of material placed between two engine parts to seal them against leaks. Gaskets are normally fiber but sometimes metal, cork, or rubber.

Glow plugs. Heating elements installed in precombustion chambers to assist in cold starting.

Governor. A device for maintaining an engine at a constant speed, regardless of changes in load.

Head gasket. The gasket between a cylinder head and a cylinder block.

Heat exchanger. A vessel containing a number of small tubes through which the engine cooling water is passed, while raw water is circulated around the outside of the tubes to carry off the engine heat.

Header tank. A small tank set above an engine on heat-exchanger-cooled systems. The header tank serves as an expansion chamber, coolant reservoir, and pressure regulator (via a pressure cap).

Hole-type nozzle. An injector nozzle with one or more very fine holes—generally used in direct (open) combustion chambers.

Horsepower. A unit of power used in rating engines.

Hunting. Cyclical changes in speed around a set point, usually caused by governor malfunction.

Hydrometer. A tool for measuring specific gravity.

Inches of mercury. A scale for measuring small pressure changes, particularly those below atmospheric pressure (i.e., vacuums).

Indicated Horsepower. The actual power developed by an engine before taking into account internal power losses.

Injection timing. The relationship of the beginning point of injection to the rotation of the crankshaft.

Injector. A device for atomizing diesel fuel and spraying it into a cylinder.

Injector nozzle. That part of an injector containing the needle valve and its seat.

Injector nut. The nut that holds a fuel line to an injector.

Intercooler. See aftercooler.

In-line pump. A series of jerk pumps in a common housing operated by a common crankshaft.

Jerk pump. A type of fuel injection pump that uses a separate pumping element for each cylinder.

Keepers. Small, dished, metal pieces that hold a valve spring assembly on a valve stem.

Lapping. A process of grinding two parts together to make an exact fit.

Lift pump. A low pressure pump that feeds diesel fuel from a tank to an injection pump.

Line contact. The machining of two mating surfaces at different angles so that they make contact only at one point.

Main bearing. A bearing within which a crankshaft rotates, and which supports the crankshaft within an engine block.

Manifold. A pipe assembly attached to an engine block that conducts air into the engine or exhaust gases out of it.

Micrometer. A tool for making precision measurements.

Naturally aspirated. Refers to an engine that draws in air solely by the action of its pistons, without the help of a supercharger or turbocharger.

Needle valve. The valve in an injector nozzle.

Nozzle body. The housing at the end of an injector that contains the needle valve.

Nozzle opening pressure. The pressure required to lift an injector needle valve off its seat so that injection can take place.

Pintle nozzle. An injector nozzle with one central hole—generally used in engines with precombustion chambers.

Piston. A pumping device used to generate pressure in a cylinder.

Piston crown. The top of a piston.

Piston pin (wrist pin). A pin connecting a piston to its connecting rod, allowing the piston to oscillate around the rod.

Piston rings. Spring-tensioned rings set in grooves in the circumference of a piston

that push out against the walls of its cylinder to make a gastight seal.

Piston-ring clamp. A tool for holding piston rings tightly in their grooves to enable them to be slipped on and off pistons.

Piston-ring groove. The slot in the circumference of a piston into which a piston ring fits.

Ports. Holes in the wall of a cylinder that allow gases in and out.

Pounds per square inch absolute (absolute pressure). Actual pressure measurements with no allowance for atmospheric pressure.

Pounds per square inch gauge (gauge pressure—psi). Pressure measurements taken with the gauge set to zero at atmospheric pressure (14.7 psi absolute).

Power train. Those components used to turn an engine's power into a propulsive force.

Pumping losses. Energy losses arising from friction in the inlet and exhaust passages of an engine.

Push rod. A metal rod used to transfer the motion of a camshaft to a rocker arm.

Pyrometer. A gauge used to measure exhaust temperatures.

Raw water. The water in which a boat is floating.

Rocker arm. A pivoted arm that operates a valve.

Rocker cover. See valve cover.

Rod-end bearing. The bearing at the crankshaft end of a connecting rod.

Scavenging. The process of replacing the spent gases of combustion with fresh air in a 2-cycle diesel.

Seizure. The process by which excessive friction brings an engine to a halt.

Sensible heat. The temperature of a body as measured by a thermometer.

Shim. A specially cut piece of shim stock used as a spacer in specific applications.

Shim stock. Very thin, accurately machined pieces of metal.

Shaft Horsepower (SHP). The actual power output of an engine and power train measured at the propeller shaft.

Slip. The difference between the theoretical movement of a propeller through the water and its actual movement.

Snap rings. Spring-tensioned rings that fit into a groove on the inside of a hollow shaft or around the outside of a shaft.

Solenoid. An electrically operated valve or switch.

Specific gravity. The density of a liquid as compared to that of water.

Speeder spring. The spring in a governor that counterbalances the centrifugal force of the flyweights.

Stroke. The movement of a piston from the bottom to the top of its cylinder.

Stuffing box. A device for making a water-tight seal around a propeller shaft at the point where it exits a boat.

Supercharger. A mechanically driven blower used to compress the inlet air.

Swept volume. The volume of a cylinder displaced by a piston in one complete stroke (i.e., from the bottom to the top of its cylinder).

Thermostat. A heat-sensitive device used to control the flow of coolant through an engine.

Thrust bearing. A bearing designed to take a load along the length of a shaft (as opposed to perpendicular to it).

Timing. The relationship of valve and fuel pump operation to the rotation of the crankshaft and to each other.

Top Dead Center (TDC). A term used to describe the position of a crankshaft when the #1 piston is at the very top of its stroke.

Torque. A twisting force applied to a shaft.

Torque wrench. A special wrench that measures the force applied to a nut or bolt.

Turbocharger. A blower driven by an engine's exhaust gas that is used to compress the inlet air.

Vacuum. Pressure below atmospheric pressure.

Valves. Devices for allowing gases in and out of a cylinder at precise moments.

Valve clearance. The gap between a valve stem and its rocker arm when the valve is fully closed.

Valve cover. The housing on an engine that is bolted over the valve mechanism.

Valve guide. A replaceable sleeve in which the valve stem fits and slides up and down.

Valve keepers. See keepers.

Valve overlap. The period of time in which an exhaust valve and inlet valve are both open.

Valve seat. The area in a cylinder head on which a valve sits in order to seal that head.

Valve spring. The spring used to hold a valve in the closed position when it is not actuated by its rocker arm.

Valve-spring clamp. A special tool to assist in removing valves from their cylinder heads.

Viscosity. The resistance to flow of a liquid (its thickness).

Volatility. The tendency of a liquid to evaporate (vaporize).

Volumetric efficiency. The efficiency with which a 4-cycle diesel engine replaces the spent gases of combustion with fresh air.

Wrist pin. See piston pin.

Yoke. The hinged and forked lever arm that couples a governor flyweight to its drive shaft.

Index